Managing College Enrollments

Don Hossler, *Editor*

NEW DIRECTIONS FOR HIGHER EDUCATION
MARTIN KRAMER, *Editor-in-Chief*

Number 53, March 1986

Paperback sourcebooks in
The Jossey-Bass Higher Education Series

Jossey-Bass Inc., Publishers
San Francisco • London

Don Hossler (Ed.).
Managing College Enrollments.
New Directions for Higher Education, no. 53.
Volume XIV, no. 1.
San Francisco: Jossey-Bass, 1986.

New Directions for Higher Education
Martin Kramer, *Editor-in-Chief*

New Directions for Higher Education is published quarterly
by Jossey-Bass Inc., Publishers (publication number USPS
990-880). *New Directions* is numbered sequentially—please
order extra copies by sequential number. The volume and issue
numbers above are included for the convenience of libraries.
Second-class postage rates are paid at San Francisco, California,
and at additional mailing offices.

Correspondence:
Subscriptions, single-issue orders, change of address notices,
undelivered copies, and other correspondence should be sent
to Subscriptions, Jossey-Bass Inc., Publishers, 433 California Street,
San Francisco, California 94104.

Editorial correspondence should be sent to the Editor-in-Chief,
Martin Kramer, 2807 Shasta Road, Berkeley, California 94708.

Library of Congress Catalog Card Number 85-81885

International Standard Serial Number ISSN 0271-0560

International Standard Book Number ISBN 87589-715-0

Cover art by WILLI BAUM

Manufactured in the United States of America

Ordering Information

The paperback sourcebooks listed below are published quarterly and can be ordered either by subscription or single-copy.

Subscriptions cost $40.00 per year for institutions, agencies, and libraries. Individuals can subscribe at the special rate of $30.00 per year *if payment is by personal check.* (Note that the full rate of $40.00 applies if payment is by institutional check, even if the subscription is designated for an individual.) Standing orders are accepted.

Single copies are available at $9.95 when payment accompanies order, and *all single-copy orders under $25.00 must include payment.* (California, New Jersey, New York, and Washington, D.C., residents please include appropriate sales tax.) For billed orders, cost per copy is $9.95 plus postage and handling. (Prices subject to change without notice.)

Bulk orders (ten or more copies) of any individual sourcebook are available at the following discounted prices: 10-49 copies, $8.95 each; 50-100 copies, $7.96 each; over 100 copies, *inquire.* Sales tax and postage and handling charges apply as for single copy orders.

To ensure correct and prompt delivery, all orders must give either the *name of an individual* or an *official purchase order number.* Please submit your order as follows:

Subscriptions: specify series and year subscription is to begin.
Single Copies: specify sourcebook code (such as, HE1) and first two words of title.

Mail orders for United States and Possessions, Latin America, Canada, Japan, Australia, and New Zealand to:
Jossey-Bass Inc., Publishers
433 California Street
San Francisco, California 94104

Mail orders for all other parts of the world to:
Jossey-Bass Limited
28 Banner Street
London EC1Y 8QE

New Directions for Higher Education Series
Martin Kramer, *Editor-in-Chief*

Contents

Editor's Notes

Demographic projections for the remaining years of this century have had an impact on colleges and universities. Institutions have become increasingly active in their search for effective organizational responses to the dilemmas posed by a declining pool of high school graduates. In the 1970s student retention and marketing were frequently the focus of attention on campuses. These efforts, however, usually operated independent of each other and often were not based on a careful analysis of the unique qualities of individual institutions and their students. In recent years some colleges and universities have attempted to develop holistic and systematic approaches to influence their enrollments. In the process a new paradigm is developing that attempts to create a "tightly coupled" enrollment management system.

This volume provides an overview of the concept of enrollment management and introduces themes related to institutional research, administrative policy, and organizational structure that are important to enrollment management efforts. On many campuses enrollment management is being equated with marketing or the general activities of the admissions office. Although these activities are an important part of enrollment management systems, the enrollment management paradigm is more comprehensive than marketing and recruitment. The assumption of the enrollment management model is that colleges and universities can engage in a set of systematic activities that will enable them to exert more direct influence over their student enrollments. Enrollment management attempts to move the locus of control for student enrollments away from a resource determined by the external environment to a resource that is more closely shaped by institutional factors. This model does not suggest that institutions of higher education can really "control" their enrollments, but the enrollment management paradigm asserts that institutions can exert more influence over their student enrollments.

In the first chapter of this sourcebook, Hossler and Kemerer provide an overview of the enrollment management concept. They define enrollment management and then describe some of the organizational elements of an enrollment management system. They also discuss the important influence of institutional research and student information systems on topics ranging from student college choice to student outcomes. Four organizational models for coordinating enrollment management activities are presented. However, the authors make it clear that any one of these models should be adapted to meet specific campus needs.

In the second chapter, Litten examines the relationship between nonprofit marketing and pricing strategies in higher education. Litten traces the evolution of marketing to the development of services marketing theory, a subtle and complex concept. The concept of services marketing and its implications for pricing policies for college and universities is just beginning to emerge. Litten analyzes these implications and raises issues for policy makers to consider.

Although many institutions express a desire to attract and retain students who will find the campus environment a satisfying and growth-producing one, there is little evidence that colleges and universities engage in systematic assessments of student needs and campus environments. Williams, in Chapter Three, presents a concise discussion of student-institution fit and outlines a step-by-step process for conducting such an assessment. He points out that student-institution fit should not be simply a matter of finding students who ''fit,'' but also one of altering the environment so that it more effectively meets the needs of students.

Bean's chapter on retaining matriculants (Chapter Four) reviews student retention from the perspective of a theory-driven model. This has frequently been missing in campus-based student retention efforts and has led to generalized programs that did not meet the needs of specific student populations. Bean helps us to understand why some retention activities seem to work and others do not, and he offers suggestions for colleges and universities who wish to develop their own attrition research programs.

In the fifth chapter, Kuh and Wallman present a summary of the outcomes of higher education. They briefly discuss methods institutions can use to assess their own outcomes. At first glance, outcomes research may seem unrelated to marketing, recruitment, and retention. However, as other chapters in this volume point out, students and parents are more attracted to campuses that have reputations for conveying more benefits to their graduates. Students are also more likely to persist when they see the utility of obtaining a degree from that institution. Kuh and Wallman include a general review of the impact of college attendance and demonstrate how one university uses its own outcomes research in marketing efforts.

Institutional research drives an enrollment management system. Davis-Van Atta and Carrier (Chapter Six) describe how institutional research can be used to help campuses understand the nature of their applicant pool and their competition for that pool of students. The authors discuss the market research questions institutions should ask at each stage of the student college choice process and how academic administrators can use this information to guide institutional policies.

In Chapter Seven, Graff examines the role of senior campus administrators in enrollment management activities. Graff poses questions for senior policy makers to consider, and he describes important roles they can play in enrollment management efforts. He emphasizes the critical role of staffing and urges institutional administrators to look for individuals with the appropriate skills rather than individuals currently holding the ''right'' titles.

Finally Claffey and Hossler suggest that enrollment management can best be understood using the imagery of a wide-angle lens. This lens allows the institution to view the student experience in a holistic manner, from the point of initial inquiry to the point of graduation. This wide-angle lens can also be used to capture the student's view of the institution. That is, by studying student perspectives of the campus before and after matriculation, faculty and administrators may be forced to see the institution as it is actually experienced, rather than as they might like to see the campus. Both perspectives can enhance student-enrollment-related policy decisions.

Don Hossler
Editor

Don Hossler is assistant professor of higher education and student affairs at Indiana University, Bloomington.

More is required than the fine tuning of recruitment practices.
Extensive reorganization may be called for.

Enrollment Management and Its Context

Don Hossler
Frank Kemerer

Many economists, demographers, public policy analysts, and education observers have projected declines in college and university enrollments. To date, however, a dramatic downturn in aggregate student enrollment figures has not occurred. Overall collegiate enrollments have remained relatively stable. The reasons for enrollment stability are varied and complex. Aggregate enrollment figures, however, mask the reality of how competitive institutions of higher education have become in their efforts to attract college students. The competition is intensifying between public and private sectors, among selective and less selective institutions, and between two- and four-year institutions. Evidence of this competition can be seen in institutional recruitment efforts and the increasing use of merit aid. It can also be seen in the lobbying activities directed toward the distribution of financial aid at the federal and state levels.

This apparent stability in enrollments, however, may be reaching its end. Federal policy efforts to reduce financial aid in a worst-case scenario may reduce the aggregate demand for higher education; at best it may result in a shift among college matriculants to less expensive higher education options. In addition, demographic projections indicate that we are about to enter a period of steeper decline in the number of traditional high school students graduating,

D. Hossler (Ed.), *Managing College Enrollments*. New Directions for
Higher Education, no. 53. San Francisco: Jossey-Bass, March 1986.

and it appears that the enrollment rates for nontraditional students may be leveling off. Since 1980, the number of returning women has risen by just 3 percent and the number of men by less than 1 percent (*Statistical Abstract of the United States: 1985*, 1984). Not surprisingly, many college administrators view this current external environment as one hostile to higher education. Nevertheless, some colleges and universities are emerging (or remaining) stronger, more vital institutions.

Institutions like Boston College, Bradley University, Carleton College, De Paul University, Oberlin College, and SUNY Geneseo have remained strong by taking a more assertive role in their efforts to attract and retain students. The organizational framework and the actions taken by these institutions vary. Some institutions have become more assertive in order to attract more students and strengthen their enrollment base. Others are more interested in exerting more influence over the types of students they seek, not wishing to grow, but rather to attract more "well-rounded" students or a more diverse student body. Despite the differing goals, there are many similarities in terms of the steps that have been taken to enable these institutions, and others like them, to have a greater impact on their student enrollments. These institutions are engaged in activities that are increasingly being referred to as enrollment management. To aid in our understanding and application of this emerging paradigm, this chapter will define enrollment management and its organizational implications.

Defining Enrollment Management

Hossler (1984, p. 6) defines enrollment management "as a process or an activity that influences the size, the shape, and the characteristics of a student body by directing institutional efforts in marketing, recruitment, and admissions, as well as pricing and financial aid. In addition, the process exerts a significant influence on academic advising, the institutional research agenda, orientation, retention studies, and student services." From a broader organizational perspective, the process inevitably leads to issues of mission and goals clarification and budgetary decision making (Kemerer and others, 1982).

Conceptually, enrollment management links research on student college choice, student-institution fit, and student attrition. Institutions that use marketing and student choice research are better able to understand their image and their competition. Choice and marketing research also enables campuses to identify their student market segments and what types of students they are most likely to attract. This information provides a mirror for institutional decision makers that enables college administrators and faculty members to see the institution as potential students see it. This can be an invaluable insight for campus administrators who frequently spend so much time articulating the institutional mission and goals to internal and external constituencies that they begin to see the institution through a filtered lens that accentuates only the positive. It may thus lead to reconsidering and sharpening the institutional mission and goals.

As a college or university begins to understand the campus image in the student marketplace, the concept of student-institution fit comes to the forefront. Which students seem to be attracted to this particular institution and where can we find them? Since institutional environments can be altered, administrators may also ask how they can change the environment so that more students will find satisfaction in attending their institution. In addition to addressing student-institution fit from the student college choice process, an enrollment management perspective also focuses on fit by means of attrition research. Student attrition studies help decision makers to understand why some students persist and why some leave the institution. Such studies typically lead to retention programs designed to improve communication between students and campus personnel, or they alter the campus environment in some way. Focusing on student persistence is also likely to enhance the fit between institution and student. This preenrollment and postenrollment analysis of student enrollment captures the unifying themes of an enrollment management system.

Organizationally there are several offices that can be part of an enrollment management system. We emphasize "can be" at this point because there is no ideal system. On each campus institutional goals, history, resources, and politics shape the nature of the enrollment management system. In addition, one of the difficulties with attempting to describe how an ideal enrollment management plan might be organized and staffed is that while some responsibilities fall neatly into existing traditional functional areas of the institution, other areas cross functional lines, which often raises territorial issues. Nevertheless, on most campuses a number of offices and responsibilities are likely to be linked formally or informally with an enrollment management system.

Successful enrollment management begins with the strategic planning process. Enrollment goals and strategies should be an important part of the planning process. Planning should illustrate how the institution sees the relationships between areas such as marketing, recruitment, student retention, academic programs, and student life. Since it is the president and other senior-level administrators who drive the planning process, one or more of the senior officers of the institution will need to understand the dimensions of an enrollment management system.

Strategic planning, as well as enrollment planning, depends on information and program evaluation. This makes the institutional research function an integral part of the enrollment management system. Market studies and retention studies provide much of the information needed to direct policy decisions. Program evaluation enables colleges and universities to assess whether or not institutional resources are being effectively utilized in enrollment-management-related programs.

Institutional research and evaluation provide much of the needed data to inform the planning process as well as direct programs in areas such as marketing and student attrition. On large campuses, an enrollment management division should ideally have its own in-house institutional researcher or policy analyst. On small campuses, the enrollment management division must have access to the institutional research office or be able to utilize faculty members with skills in research and evaluation. In many respects, planning and institutional research could be placed both at the beginning and at the end of this discussion. They are ongoing activities.

Once an institution has set its goals and objectives, the marketing and recruitment offices, typically the admissions office, must devise strategies that will present the institution in a way that is true to the traditions of the campus and that will make the campus attractive to prospective matriculants. The admissions office typically has a well-defined administrative structure; however, the nature of the activities of these offices will vary. Two-year institutions focus on a well-defined local market, but one that is characterized by a great deal of diversity. Four-year institutions draw matriculants from a much larger geographical area, but the attributes of the students are typically more homogeneous. The office of financial aid has become an important arm of marketing and recruitment efforts. As a result, the office must work closely with admissions. Ideally, the financial aid office should have developed a system for awarding aid that makes the maximum use of fiscal resources, while at the same time attracting matriculants with the kinds of characteristics the institution values. Awards should be made in a timely fashion that capitalizes on the "courtship" effects of financial aid. Research suggests that the courtship procedures institutions use to award financial aid, such as special scholarship banquets, letters from the president, and other forms of special recognition may be as important as the amount of aid in determining student matriculation.

Up to now we have focused on the elements of an enrollment management system that are responsible for attracting matriculants. Once students arrive on campus, there are a number of offices and activities that can enhance student-institution fit, success, and persistence. Academic advising and course placement, along with new student orientation, are usually among the first experiences new matriculants encounter on arrival on the campus. The sequence of these activities differs on many campuses, but they are related. The diversity of today's college students has resulted in wide variations in the interests, experiences, and skills that college students bring with them on matriculation. This has increased the importance of sound academic advising and course placement. At some less selective colleges and universities, an enrollment management plan may include placement tests that increase the likelihood of appropriate course assignments. Academic advising and orientation often set the stage for appropriate course placement, but more importantly, they help students adjust to the institution. Orientation should be designed to help students adjust to the social norms of the environment they are entering. It should help students become acclimated to the institutional environment and reduce the gap between their expectations of the campus and the realities of the institution.

Like advising and orientation, student retention research and program development usually cut across several functional lines in both academic affairs and student affairs. The difficulty with student attrition is how to organizationally manage retention program efforts. On many campuses no single office is responsible for monitoring attrition rates and implementing programs targeted at potential nonpersisters. This tends to make everyone on campus responsible for retention, yet no one truly is. The often-used and seldom effective committee approach is the frequent solution to student retention efforts. Campuses should appoint retention officers, whose primary responsibilities are to monitor student persistence rates as well as develop and evaluate retention programs. Just as financial aid and admissions have administrative structures, so should the area of student retention. The retention officer should be an integral member of the enrollment management staff.

Many colleges and universities, despite recent movements toward excellence, continue to admit some students who are underprepared for higher education. In order to help these students succeed and to reduce the likelihood that they will not persist, learning assistance centers have become part of an integrated enrollment management strategy. The center should carefully monitor the success rate of marginal students. If few of these marginally admitted students are succeeding, then the institution may not be spending recruiting and aid dollars wisely, in addition to staff time in the assistance center. There should be a feedback link between the offices of admissions, retention services, and learning assistance.

In addition to the offices and activities we have discussed thus far, the student affairs division plays a significant role in an enrollment management plan. Student activities, residence life (on residential campuses), Greek affairs, intramurals, and intercollegiate athletics play a major role in shaping the institutional environment. Policy makers need to understand the role these areas play in determining the institutional image and the educational experiences of students. The career-planning and placement function can also be an important part of an integrated enrollment management plan. Most students and parents are keenly aware of the competitive nature of the job market. Colleges that appear to place their graduates in good jobs are in a better position to attract and retain students. This function can be viewed as an element of a comprehensive enrollment management system.

The organizational activities of an enrollment management system we will address last in this section are those of institutional assessment and student outcomes research. Similar to strategic planning, institutional research and evaluation are ongoing activities that provide information and insights that can be used to drive the strategic-planning process as well as the enrollment management efforts. In order to understand the campus environment and see it as the students do, institutions need to engage in periodic assessments of students, faculty, and alumni. This could be the responsibility of the institutional research office, an administrator in academic or student affairs, or a faculty member with some release time. Like the area of campus assessment, colleges and universities should conduct studies of alumni and examine the institution's effects on students. Impact studies enable the institution to gather longitudinal data about alumni career paths as well as alumni's attitudes toward the quality of their preparation for a career and general satisfaction with their collegiate experience. This information can be used in the planning process to determine academic and student life goals.

Although enrollment management is an organizational construct, it is heavily dependent on information. This information should be derived from institutional research and sound program evaluation. Information grounds the enrollment management system in the sense that data provide the necessary perspective for sound institutional policies and informed decisions. When appropriate organizational structures are coupled with adequate resources and a data base that can provide necessary information, an enrollment management program can effectively influence the size and characteristics of student enrollments.

Organizational Models for Managing Collegiate Enrollments

Just as the specific elements of an enrollment management system vary from institution to institution, the administrative organization of their enrollment management efforts can also vary. It is important to note at the beginning that there is no one ideal organizational model. Administrators are cautioned not to adopt a model from another institution and superimpose it on an existing organizational framework. The result will be, at best, disappointment, at worst, chaos. Whatever organizational approach is used must be tailored to specific campus enrollment needs and organizational realities.

Kemerer and others (1982) have identified four archetypical models for organizing and coordinating enrollment management. The models represent a continuum in the degree of reorganization they require. At one extreme is the enrollment management committee, which requires almost no significant change. At the other extreme is the enrollment management division headed by a vice-president for enrollment management, which requires a complete overhaul of the organization chart.

The Enrollment Management Committee. The committee approach is no stranger to problem solving in higher education. If anything, it is overworked. Yet because higher education is a labor-intensive enterprise and because enrollment management must of necessity involve virtually every academic and administrative department, an enrollment management committee can go a long way to help stabilize enrollment.

The chief value of an enrollment management committee is that it can improve communication and understanding across the campus about enrollment issues. For it to maximize its potential in this regard, a committee must be broadly based, composed of representatives from academic departments, key faculty leaders, and central office administrators. Such committees are often used, but the membership is confined to those already familiar with enrollment concerns. A committee composed mainly of student affairs personnel will break down communication barriers among those offices and promote better coordination of effort, but it will have little impact on academic departments and faculty. It is the latter who must develop programs that meet student needs, disseminate materials necessary to promote them, establish relationships with feeder institutions, and assist students with degree and career planning (Kemerer, 1985).

Too often enrollment management committees end up assembling a potpourri of recommendations; then they disband. A broadly based committee headed by an effective chairperson—preferably someone other than the admissions director or student affairs administrator—can engage in a number of activities beyond those of the "wish list" variety. For example, given staff support and a budget, an enrollment management committee can conduct an assessment of current recruitment and retention activities, much in the fashion of an accreditation self-study committee. Some of the assessment can be conducted by committee members themselves. Determining faculty attitudes about campus goals and student attitudes about campus life also fall into this category. Other assessment activities such as an audit of the admissions office or of campus publications will likely require the services of an outside consultant.

An enrollment management committee can also help admissions and student affairs personnel gain cooperation from academic departments, obtain badly needed equipment or staffing, and promote the development of attractive academic courses and programs. In fact, the contributions an enrollment management committee can make are as extensive as the imagination of the person establishing it.

While the enrollment management committee is thus an inexpensive way to address enrollment problems, it does have its drawbacks. Its greatest weakness is its lack of authority. Even when structured as carefully as possible and with the best of intentions, most committees have a difficult time commanding institutional attention, even to the point of getting members to attend regularly and on time. Given these problems, an enrollment management committee is best used before an enrollment crisis occurs. Unfortunately, few colleges and universities plan ahead. Thus, the maximum value of an enrollment management committee—consciousness-raising and deliberation—is usually lost. Still, where institutional realities preclude major organizational change, an enrollment management committee can yield significant dividends.

The Enrollment Management Coordinator. One of the major problems colleges and universities have in dealing with enrollment management concerns is the lack of a central office official with responsibility in this area. It is not unusual to find that the admissions office operates largely independently of career planning and placement, the public relations office, the publications office, institutional research, and even the financial aid office. At least student recruitment has an organizational center of responsibility. Retention is a dispersed function. Everyone is responsible for retention, which means that in reality no one is.

An enrollment management coordinator is a person appointed by the president or provost to coordinate various campus activities involving student recruitment and retention. The coordinator functions in a staff position. On some campuses, the president's executive assistant is given this responsibility. The enrollment management coordinator works with unit leaders to examine goals, develop enrollment plans, coordinate efforts to achieve them, and prepare assessment programs. As a staff officer reporting to a high-level campus official, the coordinator can command sufficient visibility within the organization to act as an effective facilitator. Such a person could chair an enrollment management committee as well, thus extending his or her influence beyond the offices concerned primarily with recruitment and retention activities.

The staff coordinator model has some important advantages over a committee, the chief of which is the locus of coordination responsibility. Committees are poor coordinators. The best-developed plan can easily be squandered when it is poorly implemented. Another advantage of having a coordinator is its low cost. In most cases the person appointed to this position will already be a member of the faculty or administrative staff. But low cost is also a weakness, for the staff coordinator has no line of authority. Personality, support from top-level admimistrators, and respect from the campus community are the chief tools the staff coordinator has to get the job done. Most successful change agents need both personality and authority to be successful. Even so, the staff coordinator should not be overlooked as a potential means of resolving an enrollment problem.

The Matrix System. Some campuses have gone one step beyond the coordinator approach to introduce a matrix configuration. In effect, the matrix system augments the line responsibilities of department heads by adding a staff component. Basically, the matrix pattern involves the grouping together of independent offices into various modules. For example, offices concerned with marketing could be grouped together in a marketing module. The directors of units such as admissions, research, publications, and academic affairs could meet together as a committee to develop common goals and coordinate efforts toward their achievement. Any number of modules could be created. Thus, there could be one for recruitment, one for new student transitions, one for retention, one for assessment, and so on. The chairs of each would constitute the membership of an overarching steering committee charged with monitoring and assessing enrollment management activities for the entire campus.

The matrix approach represents more restructuring than either the committee or staff coordinator model in that individual campus units are pulled away to some degree from their regular reporting channels. Its primary advantage is that it broadens the role of unit heads by linking them with what is essentially strategic institutional planning (Kemerer and others, 1982; Cope, 1981). For large campuses, the matrix model provides a structure for diverse administrative and academic units to participate in both enrollment management and policy development activities without initiating major organizational change.

Like the other models, however, there are weaknesses in the matrix approach. The matrix is complex, and even under the best conditions there is "drag" on the system when so many disparate units are involved in a common enterprise. This is particularly true when the system is superimposed on a governance system already characterized by numerous committees and study groups. Even when the matrix system is headed by a top administrator, middle managers are more apt to follow the directives of their own superior. Faculty members are more likely to follow the requests of their chair or dean than they are proposals from a member of an enrollment management matrix module. Still, the matrix should not be overlooked as a potentially useful organizational approach to dealing with enrollment management concerns.

The Enrollment Management Division. At the opposite end of the spectrum from the committee model is the enrollment management division. As its name indicates, the division is composed of units assigned direct responsibility for some aspect of enrollment management. Thus, an enrollment management division might include admissions, registration, financial aid, publications, career planning and placement, retention, institutional research, and alumni affairs.

Rather than reporting to different administrative offices that have their own set of priorities, these units would be grouped together in a common division whose chief priority is to keep qualified students moving into and through the institution. Heading this division would be a cabinet-level vice-president. While the title may vary, the vice-president would have equal status with other vice-presidents.

The enrollment management division has one other distinct advantage over the other three models. The head of this division has the authority to secure resources and compel coordination of effort. But this model has its drawbacks, too. Political realities may preclude the extensive reorganization required to implement it. There is also often a cost factor when an experienced top-level administrator is sought to head the division. Some campuses have chosen to reconfigure the alignment of departments by converting an existing division such as student affairs into an enrollment services division. As noted at the beginning of this section, the enrollment needs of a particular campus and its organizational characteristics will play a determining role in the end product of reorganization.

It should be clear from the foregoing discussion that there is no one best system. The difficult task is to select an approach that has the greatest potential for stabilizing enrollments with the least disruption of campus life. On many campuses, there is a tendency to play down or ignore the organizational dimensions of enrollment management. Outside marketing agencies also contribute to this tendency by giving the impression that fine tuning recruitment

14

practices is all that is required. But until the internal dimensions of enrollment management are clearly understood, the success rates of the enrollment management programs and activities campus officials launch will be limited.

Concluding Observations

Enrollment management is rapidly emerging as a more comprehensive approach to directing efforts in maintaining a student body with desirable attributes that is sufficiently large to maintain institutional vitality. If it is to work, this concept must have an impact on organizational process and structures. Campus administrators must recognize that an existing model cannot be simply "lifted" from one institution and be successful. The exact structure and emphasis will vary according to the needs and history of each campus.

Enrollment management is an inaccurate term in many ways, the factors that influence collegiate enrollments are too complex to really be managed. Yet without some goals based on information and systematic cooperation among all facets of the campus, many colleges and universities may be unable to maintain stable enrollments in the future.

References

Cope, R. G. *Strategic Planning, Management, and Decision-Making.* AAHE-ERIC/Higher Education Research Report no. 9. Washington, D.C.: American Association of Higher Education, 1981.

Hossler, D. R. *Enrollment Management: An Integrated Approach.* New York: The College Board, 1984.

Kemerer, F. R. "The Role of Deans, Department Chairs, and Faculty in Enrollment Management." *The College Board Review, 1984-85, 134,* 4-8 and 28-29.

Kemerer, F. R., Baldridge, J. V., and Green, K. C. *Strategies for Effective Enrollment Management.* Washington, D.C.: American Association of State Colleges and Universities, 1982.

Statistical Abstract of the United States: 1985. Washington, D.C.: U.S. Bureau of the Census, 1984.

Don Hossler is assistant professor of higher education and student affairs at Indiana University, Bloomington.

Frank Kemerer is professor of education law at North Texas State University.

The influence of price on enrollments is not just a function of the explicit tuition charged.

Perspectives on Pricing

Larry H. Litten

The most provocative perspectives on pricing for colleges and universities have come from the introduction of marketing thought into higher education. A brief review of these developments will serve as an orientation for the consideration of pricing issues per se.

Marketing thinking slipped into higher education in the early 1970s and, by the 1980s, became an established vehicle for addressing the problems and opportunities of academic institutions. This resulted both from a quest by academic personnel for concepts and tools that would enhance academic administration and from the energetic efforts by marketers to promote their craft in new areas—health care, government and politics, the arts, and education.

Today the annual meetings of the professional associations of admissions directors, development officers, and institutional researchers and planners invariably have a number of sessions, or even an entire track, devoted to marketing and market research issues. A bibliography compiled in my office of documents either collected by ERIC or published within the past three years, contains almost four hundred items related to marketing and strategic planning in higher education. Likewise, the literatures of other nonprofit areas have blossomed with items on these topics.

The Contributions of Marketing to Higher Education

The consequences of this pull from within and this push from without were an awakening to the fact that all organizations, academic institutions not

D. Hossler (Ed.), *Managing College Enrollments*. New Directions for
Higher Education, no. 53. San Francisco: Jossey-Bass, March 1986.

excepted, are engaged in interactions with their environments and that the probabilities of accomplishing an organization's purposes can be enhanced by efforts to understand and manage these interactions effectively. As various marketers have pointed out, the issue is not *whether* to engage in marketing—since all organizations are involved in managing their interactions with markets —but whether to do it *as effectively* as marketing theory and practice permit.

Beyond an awareness that marketing is an inescapable aspect of organizational life, marketers contributed a number of basic and important concepts to the repertoire of academic administrators. They emphasized the fundamental fact that people seek to obtain something from patronizing or affiliating with an organization—the benefits that we offer are central in determining whether our institution's services are desired and by whom. Marketers also stressed the fact that it costs people something to obtain the benefits that they seek from our organizations and that these costs influence demand for our services. They summarized these two principles in a mnemonic device—the Four *P*'s. This construct stresses that an organization's relationships with its market can be influenced by what it establishes as its *products* (the benefits it offers and the means—goods or services—through which they are achieved), the *prices* of its products (the costs people must incur to achieve the benefits they seek), its *promotional* activities (how people are informed about the organization's products and their prices and how costly it is to get this information), and the *places* in which the products are available (how easy it is to obtain the product).

Marketers also taught that people usually confront a variety of options for achieving the benefits they seek; in the educational market, these options include various colleges and universities, as well as some nonacademic means of obtaining information, training, and the social and psychological benefits of higher education. Altogether, these options constitute the supply side of a market, which has a structure and in which each institution has a position. From an individual institution's perspective, these other providers of desired benefits represent the competition. Positioning to achieve a desirable place in a market via management of the Four *P*'s is a central aspect of marketing. Marketers also helped us understand that people differ in a variety of ways— the benefits they seek, the prices they are willing to pay, the means by which they obtain information and make decisions. Thus the demand side of the market consists of segments of people with particular desires or patterns of behavior. The positions of each competitor in the supply side of the market are likely to differ across segments of consumers. Segmentation, therefore, becomes an important tool for understanding the market and developing a posture on each of the Four *P*'s that establishes a desirable position for an organization within the particular segments that are important to it. Underlying all of the marketing theory relating to the ways that institutions can act in order to perform their functions most effectively is the idea that research is essential to an understanding of both sides of the market and how they interact—what people want and how they pursue their objectives and how their needs and desires are or might be fulfilled. Marketing without market research tends toward sorcery (although intuition has a respectable, if limited, place in marketing efforts). However, market research without marketing is intellectual voyeurism that brings no benefits to anyone but the researchers.

The Improved Marketing Optic of Services Marketing Theory

The emphasis on market research was the most directly beneficial and enduring legacy of the early efforts to transfer marketing thinking to higher education. Much of the early reigning theory and practice in marketing when it was first imported into higher education was simply inappropriate. It was based primarily on the marketing of consumer or industrial durables to sophisticated consumers for their private benefit. Sufficient account was not taken initially of the adolescent student consumer, confronting for the first time the selection of a complex service, with long-term private and social consequences; neither was adequate attention given to the roles of other parties who help pay for college and who influence the availability and consideration of options. A number of authors warned against an uncritical embracing of marketing (reviewed in Litten and others, 1983). Nevertheless, simplistic advice emerged concerning positioning through institutional specialization, discounted pricing schemes, overdeveloped promotional and recruiting efforts, many of which were wasteful of institutional resources and some of which were potentially damaging to the educational development of individuals or to the public interest (Lovelock and Rothschild, 1980). It was as though we were being asked to improve our vision by viewing the world through lenses ground to someone else's prescription; things were a little clearer, but they did not really come into focus.

The Emergence of Services Marketing Theory. Independently of marketing developments in higher education, marketers have rediscovered the essential distinction made by Adam Smith in the eighteenth century concerning the separate natures of goods and services. Beginning with a national conference in 1979, a distinct subspecialty has developed within the marketing profession that focuses on the marketing of services. Annual conferences devoted to services marketing are now sponsored by the American Marketing Association (AMA). The field has two newsletters and several textbooks, and a number of business schools have developed centers devoted specifically to services marketing. In 1985, the AMA published an annotated bibliography on services marketing with almost two thousand entries (Fisk and Tansuhaj, 1985).

The development of bifocals, with one lens for goods and another for services, has increased substantially the clarity of our marketing vision in higher education. Services marketing theorists have identified a number of properties of services that affect each of the Four *P*'s and the ways in which they can be employed to improve an institution's marketing effectiveness (Lovelock, 1984). Four of these properties are especially relevant to the marketing of higher education; these constitute the Four *I*'s of services marketing—intangibility, involvement, inseparability, and inconsistency.

Intangibility. Compared to goods, services are relatively difficult for the producer to promote and for the consumer to evaluate. They cannot be as directly or completely displayed or photographed; they cannot be handled, examined, compared side-by-side on a shelf or showroom floor, neither can they be "test-driven" to the same extent that physical goods can. Education is especially intangible—the teaching-learning process is difficult to observe (and describe or demonstrate); being educated is a difficult state to observe directly. Also highly intangible are the variety of developmental processes, the social and cultural benefits, that occur in conjunction with a college education.

Involvement. In many services, including higher education, the consumer must personally carry out a set of activities in order to achieve the benefits sought. Consumers often are neither trained nor skilled in the execution of these activities. They also bring varying degrees of motivation, ability, and personal resources to the task.

Inseparability. Most services are not manufactured in one highly controlled location and then delivered elsewhere for later use, as can be done with physical goods. Services are frequently produced at the same time that they are consumed, although, as in education, their benefits may be realized over a long period of time.

Inconsistency. As a consequence of the properties of involvement and inseparability, the nature and quality of services can be highly variable over time and space, even within a single organization in which many different individuals may perform a given service. Quality control is a major problem for service producers, and the judgment of quality across service providers presents major difficulties for the consumer. (While inconsistency is a major problem in the delivery of services, the flip side is the positive opportunity for the customization of the service to the needs and desires of the individual consumer—and customization can be an important marketing objective and strategy.)

Higher education possesses a number of properties that further affect how it is marketed and the marketing challenges it faces. The benefits and costs of higher education are many and complex. Both short-term (consumption) and long-term (investment) costs and benefits are relevant when a student selects a college. The costs are imposed and the benefits are realized through the actions of a variety of agents within and beyond the institution (not only the faculty and administration but other students, alumni, employers, future associates, and, to some degree, the general public). In many institutions, matriculation involves membership in a type of a club (with both the benefits and costs associated with such memberships). In many colleges and universities, matriculation is the purchase of a full system of life-support resources, a "total institution" that involves all aspects of an individual's physical, mental, and emotional well-being (again, with a considerable array of benefits and costs).

Thus, in addition to the properties that generally affect the marketing of services, higher education exhibits a number of properties that define what marketers call relatively high-risk purchases—it is expensive in a variety of ways; it is infrequently purchased (so that knowledge gained through purchase experience is absent and replacement of a given purchase is unlikely or difficult); it is of high personal importance, with long-term consequences; and its quality is difficult for the lay person to judge (indeed, difficult for the professional to judge without considerable exposure to the particular provider) (Guseman, 1981).

These several properties mean that shopping for a college education can be a relatively expensive proposition if one seeks thorough, first-hand data on several options. A student needs to understand the nature of each of several institutions, assess his or her fit with each, and then compare their relative costs and benefits (Cain and McClintock, 1984). Within each institution, exposure to too few providers (faculty, administrators, and students) or to too few beneficiaries (students and alumni) increases the risk of misjudging its costs and benefits in general and for the particular student. Theorists have postulated several consequences of these properties of services—a relative conservatism among consumers (for example, preference for well-known brands, resistance to innovations), reliance on testimonial from trusted previous users of the service or observers of its benefits, the use of indirect physical indicators of service quality (for example, appearance of the service setting and the personnel), and the use of price as a proxy for quality (Zeithaml, 1981). Both in theory and practice, these phenomena are highly applicable to the pursuit of higher education opportunities.

Pricing Research and Initiatives in Higher Education

In a market transaction, what people have to give up, that is, pay, for what they get can be an important, even a determining factor in deciding whether to obtain specific goods and services and where to go for what they seek. Pricing has been second only to promotion in the amount of attention that it is generally given during campus discussions of the various components of the Four *P*'s. A fairly large literature on price and its effects in higher education also exists.

The mid 1970s represented the *belle epoque* of this literature. A number of individuals and commissions examined the financing and pricing issues of higher education, taking into account both private and public benefits of a college education and dealing with them in terms of both equity and efficiency. Unfortunately, we have lost the broader perspectives on the discussion of pricing that prevailed then. We are no longer seeing much consideration of pricing issues with the depth and breadth that were represented in the exemplary volume published by the Carnegie Commission on Higher Education, *Higher Educa-*

tion: Who Pays? Who Benefits? Who Should Pay? (1973), and by the work of the economist Nerlove (1972). In their place today we find, on the one hand, reports and manifestos dealing with quality in education that rarely take account of either the financial or opportunity costs of their recommendations, and on the other hand, discussions of whether price discounting (merit aid) is an effective recruiting device.

Although it would be unreasonable to expect the level and type of discussion of financing and pricing issues that reigned a decade ago to be sustained without interruption, it is certainly time to resurrect it. A new generation of academic policy makers and administrators needs to examine the basic issues of equity and efficiency in the allocation of costs for higher education. Furthermore, there have been developments within and outside of academia that relate to the cost-benefit equations for both the consumption and production of higher education. The costs of producing higher education have begun to rise faster than costs in the rest of the economy (Hartle and Wabnick, 1983), even without full implementation yet of the capital-intensive technologies that could enhance the quality, and probably the long-term productivity, of colleges and universities. Major economic dislocations have occurred in the external economy, where the costs of energy have affected all sectors and the costs of housing and of public services (that is, taxes) have made increasing claims on family budgets. The social environment is rapidly changing as divorce and remarriage increasingly scramble the financial structures within which college attendance and selection decisions are made.

Recent Literature on Pricing and Its Effects. The recent literature on pricing in higher education tends to focus either on analysis of the effects of price differentials or discounting on college choice, or on the description of a limited set of pricing innovations that are under consideration or that have been implemented recently. Several seminal contributions exist, however. A nice review of methods for studying the enrollment effects of price has been prepared by Chisolm and Cohen (1982); McPherson (1978) has produced an excellent substantive review of major portions of this research. Litten (1984) contains a variety of conceptual and practical perspectives on pricing in higher education written by economists, a budget officer, a marketer, a financial aid analyst, and organizational analysts.

An important exception to the recent absence of attention given higher education pricing issues is a valuable set of papers produced for the Thirtieth Anniversary Colloquia of the College Scholarship Service. Kramer (1985) addressed some of the issues raised in the Carnegie Commission report (1973) and added new perspectives on issues regarding who should pay what for higher education.

The recent report from the Carnegie Foundation (Newman, 1985), which calls for a radical restructuring of higher education pricing, is a welcome break in the clouds that obscure the basic issues of pricing and who should pay for higher education. The arguments in the report for replacing much of the credit financing of higher education with work programs have much to commend them from an educational point of view (although the structural problems of implementing and sustaining such a system on a large scale, and integrating such opportunities into nonacademic organizations, are ignored). However, it makes less sense from an economic and productivity perspective to have students earn the money for college with the relatively low wages permitted by their unenhanced pregraduation earning power rather than with the incomes that follow graduation. (Shifting more of the burden to parents, who are relatively more productive and therefore more highly paid, makes considerable sense, even though it presents major marketing challenges.) Hearn and Longanecker (1985) provide another important recent examination of basic pricing issues from a public policy perspective.

Recent Research on Pricing. Several recent studies have examined the effects of relative prices on students' choices of colleges, although each has limited applicability due to sample characteristics.

Tierney and Davis (1985) collected data on the financial aid applicants among the high school seniors of 1979 and 1981 in Pennsylvania. Net price differentials (after subtracting aid) were a significant predictor of college choice in twenty-two out of the thirty-six socioeconomic groups examined. The researchers note further, however, that "sensitivity analysis" reveals that the behavior of these students would not be altered substantially by the levels of price movement likely to be feasible within a given sector of higher education. Tierney has further noted (private conversation, August 1985) that price sensitivity among middle-income financial white aid applicants appeared to be higher in 1981 than in 1979, following curtailment of federal financial aid programs.

In a preliminary report from a national sample of college-bound 1983 high school seniors, Chapman and Jackson (1984, p. 7) state that "monetary considerations have a small but statistically detectable influence on college choice." Their analytical model postulates that it would take a differential scholarship discount of $6,300 to raise a second-choice institution to parity with a first-choice college in probability of matriculation. As reported, however, the preliminary findings fail to take into sufficient account some of the effects of costs on choice revealed within the data (see Whitla, 1985) or of the timing of some merit-aid awards and of the nonfinancial benefits bestowed on merit-aid candidates during the admissions process, both of which can influence preferences among institutions prior to the point at which these researchers measured them.

Other research suggests that there may be substantial effects of price prior to choices among admitting institutions; indeed, Chapman and Jackson note that "the relatively modest role played by monetary considerations might well have been expected in the context of a study of college choice. Colleges which were perceived to be too expensive (even taking into account expected financial aid) were presumably ruled out of consideration during the college search phase, prior to the formation of an application set" (p. 7). Although the data come from post hoc reports by students and their parents of how they might have behaved, two studies report that price considerations drive substantial numbers of students into the public sector. Litten and others (1983) report that among high-ability students and their parents in the high school class of 1979, a concern about price was an important predictor of failure to list a private first-choice institution among students who reported a preference for private over public institutions. Furthermore, data not published previously from this study show that over two fifths of the students reported explicitly that there were institutions to which they would like to submit applications but would not because they were too costly. Similar results were reported in a national study of adults in 1983 conducted by the National Institute of Independent Colleges and Universities (1984).

An unusual series of national studies commissioned by several higher education associations has assessed general attitudes toward higher education annually since 1982. The studies included questions on the costs of higher education. The most recent report (Group Attitudes Corporation, 1984) indicates that a sizable number of people rate current tuition levels in the public sector "too high" (40 percent said they were "about right" at four-year colleges and universities, and 39 percent said they were "too high"), and a preponderant proportion held this opinion about private institutions (63 percent said they were "too high"). Furthermore, 80 percent agreed with the statement "College costs are rising at a rate that will put college out of reach of the average person in the foreseeable future." Among parents who are paying for or who expect to pay for college, 42 percent indicate that their ability to pay is a major concern. At the same time, however, this proportion has dropped slightly but steadily over the three years of the study (from 55 to 42 percent).

Recent Pricing Initiatives. In the absence of definitive findings from the research on the effects of prices on choice of college, and with marketing theory suggesting that price is important in influencing purchase decisions, academic institutions have embarked on a variety of innovations in this relatively easily manipulated component of the Four *P*'s. None of the recent pricing initiatives, however, approaches the varieties of bartering that permitted many students to achieve a higher education in America in prior centuries (Rudolph, 1962).

An extensive catalog of pricing initiatives is presented in the annual publication *Don't Miss Out; The Ambitious Student's Guide to Scholarships and Loans* (Leider, 1984). This widely distributed booklet sends an explicit signal to students that they should shop for the most attractive price and financing offerings. Advising students to develop a college selection strategy based on other factors than the possibility of rejection, the guide continues "first and foremost among these other factors should be a *consideration of the financial aid offerings.*" Students are advised to look for "innovative payment plans," "innovative aid programs," "schools with *mountains of cash,*" and "schools which enjoy *leadership in fields of study*" (order of presentation and emphasis in original). The guide lists fourteen innovative payment plans associated with twenty-two institutions. Cited are installment plans, including prepayment discounts and bonuses, tuition freezes and guaranteed tuition plans, credit card payment, electronic bank transfers, and barter arrangements. Another section lists twenty-nine innovative student aid programs associated with sixty-seven institutions. Included are subsidized loans (low interest rates or institutional payment of origination fees), family discounts (for legacies and sibling enrollment), discounts for achievements (academic, student activities, and so forth), variable tuition rates according to courses' time-of-day, employment assistance (job location, wage subsidies), and targeted scholarships for specific types of students.

Apart from the annual setting of tuition and fees, discounting arrangements probably provoke more discussion of academic pricing than any other pricing tactic. Discounting in the form of financial aid to adjust for the economic resources of families has been widely practiced for several decades; an elaborate, if somewhat arbitrary, system of needs analysis, or assessment of family financial capacity, is built into the governmental and institutional pricing practices that operate to establish the effective price for an individual student at a given college. Discounting as a means of enticing students to enroll, offered independently of family financial need (so-called merit aid), is extensive and may be on the rise. A pair of studies by the National Association of College Admissions Counselors (see Porter and McCulloch, 1984) indicates that the percentage of institutions offering no-need scholarships changed only slightly between 1982 and 1984—80 and 83 percent, respectively. In 1984, however, 76 percent indicated that the amount of dollars allocated to no-need scholarships had increased over the past three years.

Differential pricing by program within an institution according to the costs of running the specific program and its competitive position in the market has received considerable attention recently. In addition to an article on the topic (Yanikoski and Wilson, 1984), an invitational national conference was hosted by DePaul University in 1985 on this approach to higher education pricing.

Some analysts have suggested that academic institutions should "unbundle" their prices for the various functions they serve—instruction, examination, certification, counseling, recreational and cultural offerings—by charging only those who directly use each function. One law professor has accused higher education of bundled pricing of a sort that has been found illegal in other industries (Wang, 1981a, 1981b), although his arguments fail to sufficiently account for two considerations: the joint-production processes through which various functions in the list above contribute to the realization of the benefits of other functions, and the contributions that some of the functions make to the commonwealth in an academic institution (thereby justifying a tax on everyone to provide services for some from which, in turn, everyone benefits—for example, psychological counseling, medical services, or even some low-enrollment, high-cost programs that bring interesting or productive people to campus). Nevertheless, his arguments demand a careful assessment of the linkages between the various components and functions of colleges and universities, and they suggest that challenges to the present pricing practices may be in the offing.

The most far-reaching and long-lasting pricing innovations, however, are likely to come from financing and credit initiatives that protect the financial integrity of academic institutions (which can be severely compromised by many discounting schemes) but that ease the burden imposed by the financial price of higher education by spreading the payments. Zemsky, the originator of the pioneering Penn Plan at the University of Pennsylvania, has often told his audiences that "the future belongs to the financiers." Indeed, the Penn Plan, which presents a variety of options for reducing the burden imposed by the price of an education at a high-priced institution, points boldly in this direction. The Penn Plan offers alternatives for the unaided student that resemble either a fixed-rate mortgage or a variable-rate revolving credit account from which funds are drawn as needed. There are other permutations for the student with traditionally defined financial need.

If we expect, however, to move toward a system for financing higher education that is increasingly dependent on credit and debt, a number of critical issues must be researched:

Attitudes. What attitudes do students and those who influence them have toward debt? How does the general American aversion to debt, coupled with galloping use of installment credit reported by Maital (1982), relate to borrowing for education? Who sees credit as an opportunity to get a jump on the future and who sees it as increasing their risks or as compromising their future—that is, who views it as credit and who views it as debt? How is educational debt viewed in relation to other types of debt (both in its benefits and its liabilities)?

Understanding. How much do students and those who influence them understand about debt and borrowing? How complete and accurate (or realistic) are their calculations of the costs of credit, the payoffs from borrowing, the risks involved, the repayment obligations, and the relationship of educational debt repayment to other financial obligations and goals? Are different types of students more sophisticated than others when making the desirable calculations (especially, are women, with a documented mathematical deficit at the point of college entry, or minority students less sophisticated and more in need of information and counseling in these areas than their peers)?

Influence of Debt. How is debt, or its prospect, likely to influence student behavior regarding the types of institutions attended; majors selected; careers considered; postcollegiate activities such as graduate or professional school, investment in housing or business ventures, and alumni contributions?

Broadened Perspectives on Prices and Pricing in Higher Education

Although most recent research and initiatives in higher education pricing relate to the dollars costs, services marketing theory stresses that the financial price is only one of several types of personal resources involved in realizing the benefits of a college education.

The involvement of the student directly in the production of educational benefits imposes a set of nonfinancial costs. These costs can vary substantially across programs and institutions, depending on how the latter are structured, the activities they involve, the types of students they enroll, their policies governing continued participation, and the standard underlying the currency of the realm—that is, the performance levels required to obtain the symbols (for example, grades and awards) that can lead to other intrinsic benefits (for example, employment, social status). These symbols can even be translated in some instances directly into the reduction of other costs—for example, scholarships that reduce the financial price, attention from faculty or administrators that reduces various psychological costs discussed next.

Time is a major resource required in order to achieve the benefits of a college education. Time spent in educational activities cannot be spent in other activities; time spent in the program of one college cannot be spent enjoying the benefits of another institution. Effort, although related to time, is a distinct type of cost. Different levels of psychological or physical exertion can be associated with equal units of time. Programs can vary substantially in both the amount of time and the amount of effort required for completion or performance at a top level.

As "total institutions," colleges place substantial psychological and social costs on students. These costs can vary according to both the nature of the college and the background of the student. A highly religious student may experience substantial costs at a secular institution, a first-generation college-attender may experience or anticipate psychological and social costs at an institution with a strong family legacy tradition, or a student from an urban environment may view a rural institution as high in such costs.

Colleges contribute significantly to an individual's self-definition, both in his or her own eyes and in the eyes of others. A person's accomplishments in a college are a major source of this self-definition. A student's college is often used by others, however, as proxy information (regardless of its legitimacy) for a variety of less easily obtained data regarding an individual's character and social status. Admissions decisions also contribute to an individual's sense of self, especially among young adults full in the process of maturation (see Sacks, 1978).

Colleges can affect some of these psychological and social costs through their programs, structures, or policies. However, whereas financial costs tend to be relatively unambiguous, any given psychological or social phenomena may constitute benefits for one person or in one situation, but costs in another. For example, enrollment in a highly selective college may be viewed positively in some social circles, but as "putting on airs" or forsaking one's own kind in another.

Demands of the sort just discussed are a major form of direct costs. Less direct, but also part of the price, are the risks associated with pursuit of a college education. Risk is defined as the probability that the benefits desired by the student, or desired by others for or through the student (for example, by parents), will not be realized at the price that the student is willing to pay or can pay. An individual's sense of risk is a form of anxiety. Both risk and anxiety levels can be affected by the ways in which a college is structured and the ways in which it operates—all of which can be managed for marketing purposes.

In general, the lower the cost of something and the less given up to achieve a specific benefit, the better. What cost is saved can be used to achieve other desired benefits. At the same time, however, two paradoxes are associated with costs. First, as noted earlier, some psychological and social costs (for example, social pressures) may be benefits for some people (corresponding social status).

Second, when choosing a college, people may avoid low costs and may even seek relatively high costs. Often a direct association exists between price and benefit levels—some kinds of educational environments cost more than others to produce, some kinds and levels of learning necessarily require more effort than others, and some kinds of pursuits are by nature relatively risky (by our definition), regardless of cost. The reduction of costs or risks can also reduce the associated benefits. It is important for institutions to review and understand just which costs are essential for the production of given benefits and which can be reduced because they result from outdated requirements, institutional tradition or convenience, or simple inefficiency. Students, and those who influence them, should also be helped to understand the relationships between costs and benefits so that high prices are not used inappropriately simply in order to reduce the risks when purchasing a complex, professional service.

The Points at Which Costs Occur. The various types of costs just discussed occur at several points in the extended process through which a person realizes the benefits of a college education. This in turn means that the prices that institutions impose on students can be managed at corresponding points in the process.

Before College. Colleges differ from most economic enterprises in that they formally deny the opportunity to purchase to people who will have difficulty paying some of the nonfinancial prices of a particular college's program. The extent to which students have to spend time, effort, and money taking required courses or admissions tests establishes an important set of costs. Expenditures for private secondary schooling and test-coaching are the most visible and extreme costs incurred by some families in the face of selective admissions practices. Colleges can define their positions in the market in part via these preparatory prices. An institution should review its position in the market on these preparatory price dimensions and understand how these phenomena influence students' college selections (and whether some of these costs can be reduced without imposing subsequent costs on students or their future employers).

During the College Search and Selection Process. The selection of a college can be a formidable task. Choosing among the array of options can involve major investments of time, effort, and dollars in order to obtain information to make a comparative evaluation of individual institutions. The costs of considering an institution are compounded as its distance from the student's home increases (costs of visits increase, as do the costs of gaining access to people familiar with the institution). In addition to the costs of seeking and evaluating information about colleges, college selection involves the costs of completing the application—often a multistep, multiple-document, major-effort enterprise. The particular college one selects is viewed by students as having major consequences. In an unpublished Consortium on Financing Higher Education study (Litten, n.d.) of high-ability students and their parents, 50 percent of the students strongly agreed with the statement "Choosing the right college is one of the most important decisions in a person's life" (28 percent of the parents strongly agreed with this statement). Data from this same survey and from group interviews that preceded the quantitative study indicate that students are sometimes overwhelmed with the college selection task—they face an enormous set of possible choices among complex institutions claiming many benefits, and they can find it very difficult to assess how well they would match with any given institution (that is, to assess the likelihood of achieving the benefits they desire). Furthermore, given that students are making a major decision, often for the first time, and that they are still in the process of determining who they are and what they want, they face the additional risks of applying the wrong personal criteria in judging colleges, even when they can obtain credible and reliable information on each of several institutions.

These several considerations illuminate much student behavior during the college selection process, including their preferences for certain kinds of information media and their low sensitivity to financial price inducements following admission. Services marketing theory suggests that students will be quite conservative when choosing colleges and will rely on trusted informants for much information and assistance (Zeithaml, 1981). Litten and Hall (1985) have described students' preference for using friends in college for much information that serves some of the higher-level information needs of students described by Cain and McClintock (1984). Although admissions personnel may wish otherwise, friends are a rational choice of medium from the perspective of students who are managing the costs and risks of obtaining complex and often confusing information while also coping with a variety of other demands placed on them as members of families, students in high school, part-time workers, athletes, and so forth. Friends in college have more information about collegiate options than a high school student has, and they can be trusted to care about the interests of the individual student (at least more than many recruiters do). Friends can target the information they provide to the particular needs and interests of the college-seeker, whom they already know, and they afford some independent evidence regarding both the quality of the information and the college and the effects of a given college. Students rationalize, "If I know what my friend was like in high school and what he is like now, I can interpret the information I obtain from him—for example, evaluate his opinion about an institution's social life—and I can see how he has or has not changed and compare that to what I am like now and what I might become.''

Hearn and Longanecker (1985) discuss the many ways in which financial prices get buried beneath a variety of other considerations during the college selection process. Because much price discounting (for example, merit aid) comes relatively late in the college selection process, and because it constitutes only part of the price paid by students for a college education, it is not surprising that it appears to have only a modest influence, especially among students whose financial resources are not sufficiently limited so that they have ''need'' by standard calculations. After investing considerable time, money, and effort in order to investigate colleges and choose from among them (or purposely avoid such investments by choosing a familiar option), after exploiting the good will of trusted advisors and making a decision regarding available options, after reaching closure by selecting from among the many options, and after making a provisional personal identification with the chosen institution and visualizing oneself as a student there, a marginal adjustment in tuition seems like less compensation than it might to a disinterested observer (and perhaps even to the bill-paying parent).

The costs of obtaining information and of decision making are major prices that affect whether a college will be considered seriously at this critical point in the marketing process. Colleges will have to consider these elements from the cost-benefit perspective of students and those who influence them. Promotional activities cannot be designed solely from the point of view of the college and what it wants to say—they must provide some compelling information at little or no cost to consumers already overwhelmed with options and information. As a college seeks to expand beyond its primary markets, it must find ways of overcoming the costs and risks associated with the absence of ready access to the institution and to familiar sources of information (knowledgeable friends, other alumni, local reputation).

Costs During College. The financial and nonfinancial costs incurred during the time it takes to get a degree from an institution are the most visible costs of college. Therefore, I will make only brief mention of the different amounts of time and effort, as well as dollars, that institutions require. The most obvious adjustments in these costs include variations in the number of credits required for a degree, the number of hours classes meet, the amount of homework assigned per class, and the levels of performance expected in class, on papers, and in examinations. Different production technologies impose different costs on students (as well as having different types and levels of benefits)—lectures versus seminars versus independent studies as a means of producing intellectual benefits, dormitory- versus fraternity-based social life for social development, authoritarian versus democratic systems of governance for producing leadership development. Little research has been done either on the actual costs and benefits to the student associated with these alternative means of production or on the ways in which students view these costs as part of the price of an education. The nonfinancial costs of attendance can be especially important in the nontraditional adult market in which many institutions seek their salvation during the present period of contraction in the eighteen- to twenty-four-year-old market. The social and psychological costs of becoming a student during a stage in a person's life when it is not a customary role can be substantial. The costs associated with the allocation of time and effort to academic work during a period of intense demands created by the roles of employee and parent can also be formidable. At the same time, financial price differences may also be of relatively greater concern to these more mature students than to traditional students, since they have a better sense of both their specific objectives and their institutional options. These marketing problems are compounded by the presence of third-party payers (for example, employers) who can be more demanding and restrictive than parents tend to be with traditional students. Skillful marketing to this market will need to take into account this full array of prices and find ways of reducing unnecessary costs and attractively packaging others.

Costs Following College. Much of the expenditure on college is made as an investment in pursuit of benefits that follow graduation. The payoff from this investment depends in part on the skills and knowledge accumulated by the student during his or her college education and in part on how other people view the person (as well as on contacts made, networks entered, and so forth). The name of a college is used as a proxy for all manner of things associated with the institution: the kinds of students who enroll, the quality of the instruction, the resources available to students at the college, and the kinds of people who graduate from it, their levels of skill, knowledge, social status, and so forth. And, notwithstanding of our preferences, this kind of proxy information will continue to be used by employers, future acquaintances, and others (regardless of how accurate it is at the individual level) because of the costs of obtaining more explicit information, especially in the short run, when many judgments are made. Proving yourself after college, explaining where and what your college is, can be a major cost imposed on realizing the benefits of attendance, especially for colleges that are distant from the locale in which a student seeks to achieve these benefits (with some noticeable institutional exceptions that are household words). Thus, both institutional visibility and image go a long way toward establishing the price of realizing the investment made at a given college. We tend to view public relations activities as expenditures serving the interests of the institution in its efforts to attract desired resources from the market. In a real sense, however, activities that establish wider institutional visibility and that create a more concrete appreciation of a complex, rather intangible entity, are also part of the benefits package a college offers its students. Institutions should consider ways in which their public relations and alumni programs can reduce these costs to students as they design their marketing programs and establish their marketing budgets.

Where Price Fits In

Marketing impels each institution to think about both the benefits and the costs to the consumer associated with its services, to consider how its policies and practices affect these benefits and costs (and perceptions thereof), and to entertain a competitive perspective when doing so. Price appears to be an important element in the marketing equation, but the financial components of price diminish somewhat in theoretical importance when taken in the context of all the other components of the total costs incurred in order to obtain and benefit from a college education. The entire array of prices should be considered when market research is undertaken and when marketing initiatives are contemplated.

Pricing research and initiatives will need to be specific both to institutions and to market segments. General research on pricing is unlikely to illuminate sufficiently the situation and the options facing an individual institution operating in the context of a particular market with specific segments of consumers and specific competitors. Much of the ambiguity of the existing research on pricing and its effects flows from the fact that prices operate differently in different market segments. Minority students and income groups are often separated for analysis in studies of pricing and financial aid, but other important market segments have been less attended to. The children of divorced parents constitute a market segment that is growing in both absolute and relative importance in the market for higher education; it is a group that is affected critically by pricing policies. An extensive longitudinal study of families with divorced parents documents the substantial difficulties that surround college attendance for children in these circumstances (Wallerstein and Corbin, forthcoming). Pursuing price discounts via financial aid can compound these difficulties, imposing severe psychological costs cn the participants. In the many instances in which contributions should be expected from both parents, the aid process requires sharing financial data and achieving agreements between parties who are established adversaries. This may well produce a disinclination among such students to consider higher-priced collegiate options. Some institutions impose greater costs in this area than others by the ways in which they communicate family contributions (that is, as a single sum instead of as separate amounts for each parent). Higher education marketers are going to have to confront the pricing and payment implications of the escalating dislocations caused by divorce, especially in the tuition-dependent private sector.

Equally important as price, if not more important, are the benefits offered by an institution and how they compare with the benefits offered by competitors. Research conducted by the Strategic Planning Institute (Buzzell and Wiersema, 1981) suggests that in the "mature" industries represented in their data base derived from almost two thousand businesses, companies rarely attempt to improve their market shares by means of price reductions. (Universities, one of the two social institutions surviving from the medieval era, certainly constitute a mature industry.) Price reductions are too easily matched by competitors. Instead, in order to increase market shares, these firms rely on promotional (information-providing) activities, new products, and improvements in product quality—that is, in the benefits offered—derived from less readily matched research and development.

These findings should be instructive. As we look beyond the boundaries of our own industry for insights produced within the marketing profession and discipline, we should strive to learn from the most successful of these secular marketers. At the same time, we must recognize that the nature of our enterprise presents some major challenges. In education—an intangible, complex, professional service, with both investment and consumption benefits—it is not easy to demonstrate quality, especially differential levels of quality, in ways that are responsible as well as credible and persuasive to the relatively unsophisticated lay markets that we seek to serve. Nevertheless, it is in the enhancement of quality that the benefits to society and to individual students are located; it is also where the long-term marketing advantages for individual institutions are likely to lie. Certainly a major ethical obligation for institutions is to avoid exploiting financial price as a specious indicator of institutional quality.

This is not to suggest that concern about financial price is misdirected. Indeed, we should seek to reduce unnecessary costs, to allocate costs equitably according to where benefits are realized, and to understand and communicate essential linkages between specific costs—financial and otherwise—and specific benefits. At the same time, however, we must place our concern for the financial cost in proper perspective. Equal or greater attention should be given to the benefits we provide and to the entire array of costs that impinge on the desires and capacities of students and their families to pursue a college education as well as to meet the demands of their other social and economic roles.

References

Buzzell, R. D., and Wiersema, F. D. "Successful Share-Building Strategies." *Harvard Business Review*, 1981, *59* (1), 135–144.

Cain, P. P., and McClintock, J. "The ABC's of Choice." *The Journal of College Admissions*, 1984, *105*, 15–21.

Carnegie Commission on Higher Education. *Higher Education: Who Pays? Who Benefits? Who Should Pay?* New York: McGraw-Hill, 1973.

Chapman, R. G., and Jackson, R. "The Influence of No-Need Financial Aid Awards on the College Choices of High-Ability Students." Paper presented to the annual meeting of the College Board, New York, Oct. 1984.

Chisolm, M., and Cohen, B. *A Review and Introduction to Higher Education Response Studies.* Boulder, Colo.: National Center for Higher Education Management Systems, 1982.

Fisk, R. P., and Tansuhaj, P. S. *Services Marketing—An Annotated Bibliography.* Chicago: American Marketing Association, 1985.

Group Attitudes Corporation. *American Attitudes Toward Higher Education, 1984.* New York: Group Attitudes Corporation, 1984.

Guseman, D. S. "Risk Perception and Risk Reduction in Consumer Services." In J. H.

Donnelly and W. R. George (Eds.), *Marketing of Services*. Chicago: American Marketing Association. 1981.

Hartle, T. W., and Wabnick, R. "Are College Costs Rising?" *Journal of Contemporary Issues*, 1983, *1* (2), 63–71.

Hearn, J. C., and Longanecker, D. "Enrollment Effects of Alternative Postsecondary Pricing Policies." *Journal of Higher Education*, 1985, *56* (5), 485–508.

Kramer, M. A. "The Costs of Higher Education: Who Pays and Who Should Pay?" In College Scholarship Services, *An Agenda for the Year 2000*. New York: College Entrance Examination Board, 1985.

Leider, R. *Don't Miss Out; The Ambitious Student's Guide to Scholarships and Loans*. Alexandria, Va.: Octameron Associates, 1984.

Litten, L. H. (Ed.). *Issues in Pricing Undergraduate Education*. New Directions for Institutional Research, no. 42. San Francisco: Jossey-Bass, 1984.

Litten, L. H. *Report from Market Research Project*. Consortium on Financing Higher Education, Cambridge, Mass., n.d.

Litten, L. H., and Hall, A. E. "Preferred Sources of Information Among Students Who Are Searching for Colleges." Unpublished paper, the Consortium on Financing Higher Education, Cambridge, Mass., 1985.

Litten, L. H., Sullivan, D., and Brodigan, D. L. *Applying Market Research in College Admissions*. New York: College Entrance Examination Board, 1983.

Lovelock, C. H. *Services Marketing*. Englewood Cliffs, N.J.: Prentice-Hall, 1984.

Lovelock, C. H., and Rothschild, M. L. "Uses, Abuses, and Misuses of Marketing in Higher Education." In The College Board (Ed.), *Marketing in Higher Education: A Broadening of Perspectives*. New York: College Entrance Examination Board, 1980.

McPherson, M., "The Demand for Private Education." In C. Finn and D. Breneman (Eds.), *Public Policy in Private Higher Education*. Washington, D.C.: Brookings Institute, 1978.

Maital, S. *Minds, Markets, and Money—Psychological Foundations of Economic Behavior*. New York: Basic Books, 1982.

National Institute of Independent Colleges and Universities. *A National Study on Parental Savings for Children's Higher Education Expenses*. Washington, D.C.: National Institute of Independent Colleges and Universities, 1984.

Nerlove, M. "On Tuition and the Costs of Higher Education: Prologomena to a Conceptual Framework." In T. Schultz (Ed.), *Investment in Higher Education*. Chicago: University of Chicago Press, 1972.

Newman, F. *Higher Education and the American Resurgence*. Princeton, N.J.: Princeton University Press, 1985.

Porter, B. A., and McColloch, S. K. *The Use of No-Need Academic Scholarships: An Update*. Skokie, Ill.: National Association of College Admissions Counselors, 1984.

Rudolph, F. *The American College and University*. New York: Knopf, 1962.

Sacks, H. S. "Bloody Monday: The Crisis of the High School Senior." In H. S. Sacks and Associates, *Hurdles: The Admissions Dilemma in American Higher Education*. New York: Atheneum, 1978.

Tierney, M. L., and Davis, J. S. "The Impact of Student Financial Aid and Institutional Net Price on the College Choice Decisions of In-State Seniors." *Journal of Student Financial Aid*, 1985, *15* (1), 3–20.

Wallerstein, J., and Corbin, S. "Children of Divorce: Educational Opportunities and Attainment Ten Years Later." *Family Law Quarterly*, forthcoming.

Wang, W. K. S. "The Beginnings of Dismantling." *Improving College and University Teaching*, 1981a, *29* (3), 115–121.

Wang, W. K. S. "The Dismantling of Higher Education." *Improving College and University Teaching*, 1981b, *29* (2), 55–60.

Whitla, D. K. "A Retrospective Glance at Admissions Issues—The Harvard Summer Institute at 25." *College Board Review*, 1985, *135*, 7-8, 38-40.

Yanikoski, R. A., and Wilson, R. F. "Differential Pricing of Undergraduate Education." *Journal of Higher Education*, 1984, *55* (6), 735-750.

Zeithaml, V. "How Consumer Evaluation Processes Differ Between Goods and Services." In J. H. Donnelly and W. R. George (eds.), *Marketing of Services.* Chicago: American Marketing Association, 1981.

Larry H. Litten is associate director and director of research at the Consortium on Financing Higher Education, Cambridge, Massachusetts.

Students will enroll and remain enrolled in colleges that offer opportunities and support that match their needs.

Optimizing Student-Institution Fit

Terry E. Williams

The critical task of managing student enrollments in higher education must necessarily involve much more than marketing the institution and the subsequent recruitment of new students to the campus. Hossler (1984, 1985), Kemerer and others (1982), and other authors have all agreed that effective enrollment management must include a coordinated and well-conceived campus-wide effort that results in a systematic focus not only on the critical recruitment effort but also on strategies and plans to retain students once they have matriculated.

This chapter focuses on an important concept that affects and at the same time is affected by both an institution's recruitment and its retention efforts. This concept, commonly referred to as *student-institution fit*, is not new to higher education, since many admission officers have for years been concerned with fitting, or matching, student characteristics with institutional characteristics, believing that a good match will result in satisfied and productive graduates for the institution. What is new, however, is that enrollment managers today must use an interactionist-based process that will result in positive action to significantly increase the fit between students and institution. This effort to fit student with institution clearly must be woven into both campus recruitment and marketing plans as well as campus-wide retention programs.

This chapter specifically clarifies the concept of student-institution fit in higher education and the broader conceptual foundation on which it is based. The primary aim of the chapter is to link the concept of fit to enrollment management by presenting a new process model for operationalizing the conceptual

D. Hossler (Ed.), *Managing College Enrollments.* New Directions for Higher Education, no. 53. San Francisco: Jossey-Bass, March 1986.

and theoretical constructs such that levels of fit between student and campus can be more effectively managed. This process model includes five action steps: assessing entering student characteristics, assessing the characteristics of the campus environment, identifying levels of student-institution fit, evaluating levels of fit, and designing environmental interventions.

Student-Institution Fit Clarified

In understanding the concept of student-institution fit, enrollment managers should carefully consider three important sets of variables: characteristics of students, characteristics of the institutional environment, and the effects or outcomes resulting from the interaction of the student with the campus environment. For example, student characteristics include such personal attributes as goals, abilities, needs, interests, values, and expectations. Institutional characteristics include a wide array of physical, academic, social, and psychological variables that together comprise the campus environment. Finally, the interactions between students and campus environment affect students' physical behavior, their cognitive filtering of what they are experiencing, and in the affective domain, their perceptions and attitudes toward the campus environment. These interaction effects constitute an important student-institution relationship that affects to varying degrees student satisfaction, academic achievement, and persistence in the institution. When student goals, needs, interests, values, and expectations are adequately met within the campus environment, then from the student perspective, a certain degree of fit or congruency exists. Likewise, when the student's academic and social abilities seem to mesh well with campus requirements, the fit or match between student and institution is also believed to exist.

Enrollment managers on the campus, who must persuasively present to faculty and management groups this notion of matching students with institution for both recruitment and retention purposes, have a significant body of theory- and research-based literature for support. Several studies conducted over the past thirty years have specifically focused on variables related to student-institution fit. For example, twenty years ago researchers found that congruency between student expectations for the college environment and their actual perceptions of the environment strongly correlate with positive student adjustment to the campus and even with academic achievement (Lauterbach and Vielhaber, 1966). Another researcher found that a campus housing policy of putting large numbers of students with similar majors on the same residence hall floors also exerted a significant impact on student feelings about academic major, college satisfaction, and even social interaction (Brown, 1968). In this study, those students with academic majors not a part of the numerically dominant group reported significantly more dissatisfaction not only with their housing arrangements but with their overall college experience as well. Congruency between personality type and academic major has also been found to correlate with significantly greater student satisfaction on the campus (Morrow, 1971; Nafziger and others, 1975). Other studies have also correlated student-institution fit with student satisfaction and achievement and have obtained similar results (Pervin, 1967; Walsh and Russell, 1969; Starr and others, 1972). In summary, the research literature does reveal agreement among many scholars who support the link between student-institution fit and increased levels of student satisfaction with the institution, academic achievement, and personal growth (Walsh, 1978; Huebner, 1980; Lenning and others, 1980).

Student-Campus Interaction: A Conceptual Foundation

In order for enrollment managers to be fully cognizant of both student and campus factors influencing fit, they must also be familiar with the theoretical framework on which the concept of fit is established. This framework consists of a family of theory-based models that should be an integral part of the professional preparation of those seeking to serve a leadership role in enrollment planning in higher education. For those on the campus who have this role thrust on them, continuing education through graduate coursework or focused seminars should be sought.

Student-institution fit is directly related to a broad theoretical concept known as person-environment interaction. The application of this concept to higher education has recently been the focus of much attention as more and more administrators learn about and subscribe to the campus ecology movement now sweeping higher education. This movement, of which enrollment management is an important part, emphasizes not just how to help students adapt to their college or university environment but also how to adapt the campus environment to students.

Theorists and researchers, especially from the fields of psychology and sociology dating back to 1924, have explored the relationships between individuals and their environments. Kantor (1924), Lewin (1936), and Murray (1938) were each early contributors to the theoretical foundation for interactionism. The importance of understanding factors that contribute to person-environment interaction becomes clearer if one assumes that all aspects of human behavior—what one knows, feels, and does—cannot occur in a vacuum. Not only do people bring their own physical, social, and psychological characteristics into the environment but the environment in which they live necessarily has an impact and influence on their behavior. Thus, the interactionist perspective would suggest that both the individual and the environment shape each other. It is this perspective that serves as the link between enrollment managers and their understanding of student-institution fit. Several reviews of theory-based models of person-environment interaction are available that hold particular value for enrollment managers. The reader is encouraged to turn to these sources for an introduction to the theory base (see Walsh, 1973, 1975, 1978; Huebner, 1979, 1980; and Williams, 1984).

A Model for Optimizing Student-Institution Fit

It has been shown that research supports the interactionist theory that posits that congruency, or fit, between students and their campus environment can lead to higher levels of satisfaction and academic achievement. The remaining sections of this chapter describe how those with responsibility for enrollment planning on the campus can effectively operationalize the conceptual constructs in order to optimize the fit between campus and student.

In order to systematically increase the fit, or match, between student and campus, I propose a five-step process model. The model can serve as an important starting point for any campus enrollment management team in that it outlines five basic sets of tasks that together facilitate not only the assessment of current levels of fit between student and campus but also the design of strategies for increasing or optimizing levels of fit. The five action steps in the model include: assessing student characteristics, assessing environmental characteristics, identifying the fit between student and institution, evaluating levels of fit, and designing environmental interventions. Each of these steps is described in the sections that follow.

Assessing Student Characteristics. As was described earlier, the first of three factors affecting levels of student-institution fit consists of diverse personal attributes that students bring with them to the campus, such as their academic achievements and abilities, their personal and career-related goals, special needs they may have, and their expectations about various aspects of campus life. The first step in the process model thus requires the institution to systematically collect a wide variety of demographic and perceptual data on all students at the time of their matriculation. This would include new freshmen as well as transfer students. Those campuses with graduate and professional programs should also consider collecting similar data for these advanced students.

The enrollment management team should establish the types of data to be collected. However, it is best to collect as much information on each student as possible. Several types of demographic data can be compiled by accessing campus admissions records. Perceptual data about student attitudes, values, and expectations can be collected either with local instruments designed by the institution or with standardized instruments such as those designed by the American College Testing Program or the National Center for Higher Education Management Systems. These instruments are designed especially for entering students and collect both demographic and perceptual data.

Traditionally, a large amount of demographic data has been routinely collected on new students, but very little seems to be done to assess student attitudes, values, and expectations at the time of entry. For example, an enrollment management team should know what goals and expectations new students bring with them to the campus in order to ascertain whether or not these goals and expectations are realistic ones that can reasonably be met within the campus environment. A major source of new student dissatisfaction with a campus often arises as a result of unfulfilled expectations. This first step in the model also involves determining what factors have significantly influenced the goals and expectations of entering students, especially focusing on environmental referants for those goals that may be unrealistic. For example, if students enter with perhaps unrealistic expectations regarding the quality (and frequency) of student-faculty interaction outside the classroom, then it would be important to ascertain just how these expectations were reinforced. The findings may lead the campus enrollment management team to recommend that immediate changes be made in order to reduce the number of misconceptions being communicated to prospective students.

Assessing Environmental Characteristics. The second of the three factors that influence levels of fit between institution and student consists of the complex variables that together comprise the campus environment. Just as it is important for enrollment managers to fully understand the many characteristics that make up the student population, they must also clearly understand their own campus environment before they can begin to assess the impact it has on students. This analysis of the campus environment constitutes the model's second step.

In recent years researchers have proposed varying ways of conceptualizing and defining campus environments (see Astin, 1968; Banning and McKinley, 1980; Blocher, 1974, 1978; and Moos, 1974). Even though each approach is unique, each in some way focuses on four broad domains that comprise the campus environment: an academic-intellectual domain, a physical domain, a social-cultural domain, and a psychological domain. Although it is possible to characterize individual factors contributing to each of the four domains, one must remember that overlap does exist between the domains. For example, the lighting of campus buildings and walkways is obviously a part of the physical environment; however, the absence of adequate lighting could also affect the psychological, academic, and social environments because poor lighting could create in students a fear for their personal safety, which, in turn, could reduce student evening use of a library, reduce night class enrollments, or reduce participation in evening social events.

Another important set of characteristics of the overall campus environment that is often overlooked and that also affects all four environmental domains includes institutional values, goals, and objectives. The educational philosophy, values, and goals that serve as the basic foundation on which the institution's core programs and activities are based are an important part of the campus environment. The identification of these values and goals is essential if an institution is to have reliable standards against which to compare the effects, or outcomes, arising from the interaction of student characteristics with institutional characteristics. The process of determining institutional values, goals, and objectives should be one that involves in meaningful ways all campus constituencies. The entire campus community, including constituencies external to the institution, such as prospective students and their parents, should be made fully aware of the institution's specific values and goals. Kuh and others (1984), in addressing the need to communicate clearly to prospective students factors contributing to institutional quality, state that "institutions with a clear, salient purpose . . . can more persuasively demonstrate quality than institutions with ambiguous purposes" (p. 172).

A wide variety of tools are available for assessing the campus environment. Huebner (1980) reviews four general approaches to environmental assessment. These include demographic, perceptual, behavioral, and multimethod approaches. The demographic method is objective and descriptive and focuses on variables that are fairly easy to measure: physical size of campus buildings, numbers of faculty and staff, ratio of students to faculty, and size of library holdings. Astin and Holland (1961) and Holland (1971) have designed demographic instruments for use in environmental assessment. It is entirely feasible for a campus enrollment management team to design its own local instruments in collecting needed demographic data. Perceptual tools are the best developed and most widely used of the four types. Frequently used instruments include the Classroom Environment Scale (Moos and Trickett, 1976), the University Residence Environment Scale (Moos and Gerst, 1976), the College Characteristics Index (Pace and Stern, 1958), the Organizational Climate Index (Stern, 1970), the College and University Environment Scales (Pace, 1969), the Student Opinion Survey (American College Testing Program, 1984), and the Institutional Goals Inventory (Educational Testing Service, 1972).

The behavioral approach to assessment measures specific, observable behaviors of students, faculty, or staff. Although this approach is not well developed, some measures are available: the Inventory of College Activities (Astin, 1971) and the Experience of College Questionnaire (McDowell and Chickering, 1967). The fourth assessment type combines all three of the previous methods in an effort to collect a wide variety of data in a single assessment (see Peterson's, 1968, College Student Questionnaire and Centra's, 1970, Questionnaire on Student and College Characteristics).

Identifying the Fit Between Student and Institution. The third and final element of student-institution fit involves considering the effects of the interaction between the student and the campus environment. This would include investigating not only how the environment has both positively and negatively affected the student but also how student involvement in the institution has influenced the environment. The process of identifying fit between student and campus includes recording where apparent matches and mismatches have occurred. This identification process thus constitutes the third step in the model.

To begin this process, it is perhaps easier to identify where mismatches have occurred between student and campus. Often these mismatches become apparent when students experience academic, social, and other personal adjustment problems while enrolled at the institution. It is essential that a reporting system be established that will channel information from all sections of the campus regarding the nature and frequency of problems experienced by students to one central location (such as the enrollment management team) for careful analysis. It is not as important at this point to know the identity of those students with problems as it is to know generally the types of issues, concerns, needs, and problems that students are having as well as those that students themselves identify.

Student perceptions of the campus environment thus need to be collected on a regular basis, and, as was noted earlier, several perceptual and behavioral assessment tools are available. However, a special focus should be directed toward determining the environmental referants that students indicate most influence their views. Those students who leave the institution before graduation and thus become a part of campus attrition statistics are often the ones who are most dissatisfied with some aspect of the campus. Many of these students express feelings of being in the wrong place at the wrong time and of being mismatched with campus expectations or norms. To illustrate, Painter and Painter (1982) describe four examples of student-reported mismatches with the campus: (1) incongruence between students' prior expectations about campus life and what they actually experience on the campus, (2) inadequate opportunities to develop close friendships with peers of similar backgrounds, (3) lack of fit between student academic abilities and faculty expectations for their work, and (4) the apparent inability of the institution to meet student career-related, recreational, and other general support needs.

Much activity now taking place in American higher education to develop new institutional strategies for student retention involves the investigation of the many complex factors that influence student decisions to leave the institution. These research and program evaluation studies are a crucial part of an institution's assessment of matches and mismatches between student and campus. A wealth of information is collected in these studies, which can be used by the enrollment management team to identify where mismatches exist between students needs, expectations, and goals and institutional abilities to respond effectively to these needs, expectations, and goals. Since these studies are often of the "autopsy" nature (Terenzini, 1982) in that they focus entirely on students who have terminated enrollment, it is still very important that current students be assessed on a regular basis in order to collect data on potential sources of mismatches or mismatches in the making. Often students will persist in a college environment while at the same time feeling very dissatisfied with some aspect of that environment.

Thus far this discussion of assessing fit between student and campus has focused on the need to identify mismatches and sources of student dissatisfaction with the campus environment. It is just as important for an enrollment management team to identify what students seem to enjoy most about the campus and those environmental factors that appear to match well with student needs, goals, interests, and expectations. The campus certainly should be most interested in surveying and interviewing student persisters, especially at or near graduation time. Alumni who are supportive of institutional requests for financial assistance, as well as those who volunteer their services in the institution's recruitment and placement activities, should also be regularly contacted for their perceptions of the campus environment.

Evaluating Levels of Fit. The fourth step in the process model involves evaluation and analysis of the data collected through Step 3. The primary objective of this step is to enable the enrollment management team or other institutional officers to make important decisions regarding whether or not to proceed with a plan for an intervention that would reduce mismatches between student and campus. A major assumption underlying this evaluative step is that not all mismatches can or even should be corrected through special interventions. It is probable that some mismatches may involve variables totally out of the control of the institution. After careful evaluation, the institution may also find that a potential solution, or intervention, for a mismatch between one group of students and the campus may in itself lead to a more serious problem with another group of students. Therefore, the evaluation component is a most important step in this process model that must not be undervalued.

The evaluation process begins with the enrollment management team devising some plan for systematically evaluating the data. For example, a procedure could be established whereby recorded matches and mismatches are each placed at some point on a continuum that indicates type and intensity of impact or effect on the institution. This continuum could range from "very negative impact" to "very positive impact." In assigning match-mismatch incidents to the continuum, the enrollment team needs to consider a variety of factors that affect the direction and intensity of the impact. For example, the institution could determine from the data the approximate number of students who are directly involved. It seems reasonable to expect that the greater the number of students experiencing a particular problem, the more concerned the institution should be. However, if only a few students seem to be involved, this must also be weighed carefully. One should be cautious about arbitrarily determining levels of impact based solely on the number of affected students. It could very well occur that a small number of students, who also represent a significant percentage of a student subculture (such as minority students), could be experiencing problems arising from a poor fit with some aspect of the campus. In this instance the institution should not ignore this data even though a small number of students have been affected. Other factors might also be considered in evaluating the impact on the institution of matches and mismatches. Some of these might include assessing levels of student satisfaction and dissatisfaction arising from the match or mismatch, assessing what correlation exists between a match or mismatch and student persistence or attrition in the institution, and determining to what degree the match or mismatch either supports or impedes the institution in fulfilling its stated educational goals and objectives.

Designing Environmental Interventions. If the comprehensive evaluation undertaken by the enrollment management team in Step 4 of this model leads to decisions to move forward with specific programs aimed at effectively reducing levels of mismatches between student and campus, then the fifth and final step in the model is taken. In this step an enrollment team considers as valid not only those interventions that focus on assisting students to adjust to or to cope with the campus environment but also interventions that focus on adapting or changing the campus environment to meet the needs, interests, goals, and expectations of students.

The traditional approach taken by institutions of higher education in reacting to apparent mismatches between student and campus has been to immediately assume that something is wrong with the student, since he or she has not been able to effectively adjust to the demands of the collegiate environment. This long-standing view thus considered students as deficient in some way and therefore in need of direct personal or academic intervention (Banning and McKinley, 1980). The resulting interventions usually included getting the student to see either an on-campus counselor or removing the student physically from the campus either through a judiciary process or at times by arbitrarily withdrawing the student for a variety of ill-defined mental health reasons (Pavela, 1985). While direct interventions on a one-to-one basis may at times be valid and in the best interests of both the student and the campus, an institution should not solely rely on this approach in trying to reduce the number of incidents of mismatches between student and campus. Banning and Kaiser (1974) state that if the institution always assumes that students are deficient in some way when they experience problems while on the campus, then institutional efforts may at times be inappropriately directed at helping students adjust to a deficient campus environment.

A variety of interactionist process models are available that specifically focus on environmental intervention. These can be especially valuable to enrollment management teams as they plan and implement interventions at three different levels: focusing on individual students (life-space level), focusing on selected groups of students (microlevel), and focusing campuswide (macrolevel). Readers desiring more detailed information about these models should review Huebner and Corrazzini, 1976; Kaiser, 1978; Miller and Prince, 1976; Morrill and others, 1980.

Conclusion

A substantial research base exists to support the notion that a good match, or fit, between student abilities, interests, goals, needs, and expectations and the institution's ability to adequately respond to those interests, needs, and so on, leads to higher levels of student satisfaction with the campus and higher levels of academic achievement as well. Effective enrollment management thus demands that campus enrollment planners fully understand not only student characteristics and campus characteristics but also the behavioral, cognitive, and affective outcomes resulting from the interaction of students with their campus environment.

References

American College Testing Program. *Student Opinion Survey.* Iowa City, Ia.: American College Testing Program, 1984.

Astin, A. W. *The College Environment.* Washington, D.C.: American Council on Education, 1968.

Astin, A. W. "Two Approaches to Measuring Students' Perceptions of Their College Environment." *Journal of College Student Personnel*, 1971, *12*, 169–172.

Astin, A. W., and Holland, J. L. "The Environmental Assessment Technique: A Way to Measure College Environments." *Journal of Educational Psychology*, 1961, *52*, 308–316.

Banning, J. H., and Kaiser, L. "An Ecological Perspective and Model for Campus Design." *Personnel and Guidance Journal*, 1974, *52*, 370–375.

Banning, J. H., and McKinley, D. L. "Conceptions of the Campus Environment." In W. H. Morrill, J. C. Hurst, and E. R. Oetting (Eds.), *Dimensions of Intervention for Student Development.* New York: Wiley, 1980.

Blocher, D. H. "Toward an Ecology of Student Development." *Personnel and Guidance Journal*, 1974, *52*, 360–365.

Blocher, D. H. "Campus Learning Environments and the Ecology of Student Development." In J. H. Banning (Ed.), *Campus Ecology: A Perspective for Student Affairs.* Cincinnati, Oh.: National Association for Student Personnel Administrators, 1978.

Brown, R. D. "Manipulation of the Environmental Press in a College Residence Hall." *Personnel and Guidance Journal*, 1968, *46*, 555–560.

Centra, J. A. "The College Environment Revisited: Current Descriptions and a Comparison of Three Methods of Assessment." *College Entrance Examination Board Research and Development Reports.* RDR-70-71, no. 1. Princeton, N.J.: Educational Testing Service, 1970.

Educational Testing Service. *The Institutional Goals Inventory.* Princeton, N.J.: Educational Testing Service, 1972.

Holland, J. L. *The Self-Directed Search.* Palo Alto, Calif.: Consulting Psychologists Press, 1971.

Hossler, D. R. *Enrollment Management: An Integrated Approach.* New York: The College Board, 1984.

Hossler, D. R. "Enrollment Management: A Paradigm for Student Affairs Professionals." *NASPA Journal*, 1985, *23* (2), 2–8.

Huebner, L. A. (Ed.). *Redesigning Campus Environments.* New Directions for Student Services, no. 8. San Francisco: Jossey-Bass, 1979.

Huebner, L. A. "Interaction of Student and Campus." In U. Delworth, G. R. Hanson, and Associates (Eds.), *Student Services: A Handbook for the Profession.* San Francisco: Jossey-Bass, 1980.

Huebner, L. A., and Corrazzini, J. G. "Ecomapping: A Dynamic Model for Interventional Campus Design." *Student Development Staff Papers, no. 6.* Fort Collins: Colorado State University, 1976.

Kaiser, L. R. "Campus Ecology and Campus Design." In J. H. Banning (Ed.), *Campus Ecology: A Perspective for Student Affairs.* Cincinnati, Oh.: National Association for Student Personnel Administrators, 1978.

Kantor, J. R. *Principles of Psychology*, Vol. 1. Bloomington, Ind.: Principia Press, 1924.

Kemerer, F. R., Baldridge, J. V., and Green, K. C. *Strategies for Effective Enrollment Management.* Washington, D.C.: American Association of State Colleges and Universities, 1982.

Kuh, G. D., Coomes, M. D., and Lundquist, I. A. "What Prospective Students Really Need to Know About Institutional Quality." *College and University*, 1984, *59*, 167–175.

Lauterbach, C. G., and Vielhaber, D. P. "Need-Press and Expectation-Press Indices

45

as Predictors of College Achievement." *Educational and Psychological Measurement*, 1966, *26*, 965–972.

Lenning, O. T., Sauer, K., and Beal, P. E. *Student Retention Strategies*. AAHE-ERIC/ Higher Education Research Report no. 8. Washington, D.C.: American Association for Higher Education, 1980.

Lewin, K. *Principles of Topological Psychology*. New York: McGraw-Hill, 1936.

McDowell, J. V., and Chickering, A. W. *The Experience of College Questionnaire*. Plainfield, Vt.: Project on Student Development, 1967.

Miller, T. K., and Prince, J. S. *The Future of Student Affairs: A Guide to Student Development for Tomorrow's Higher Education*. San Francisco: Jossey-Bass, 1976.

Moos, R. H. "Systems for the Assessment and Classifications of Human Environments: An Overview." In R. H. Moos and P. Insel (Eds.), *Issues in Social Ecology*. Palo Alto, Calif.: National Press Books, 1974.

Moos, R. H., and Gerst, M. *University Residence Environment Scale Manual*. Palo Alto, Calif.: Consulting Psychologists Press, 1976.

Moos, R. H., and Trickett, E. *Classroom Environment Scale Manual*. Palo Alto, Calif.: Consulting Psychologists Press, 1976.

Morrill, W. H., Hurst, J. C., and Oetting, E. R. (Eds.). *Dimensions of Intervention for Student Development*. New York: Wiley, 1980.

Morrow, J. M., Jr. "A Test of Holland's Theory of Vocational Choice." *Journal of Counseling Psychology*, 1971, *18*, 422–425.

Murray, H. A. *Explorations in Personality*. New York: Oxford University Press, 1938.

Nafziger, D. H., Holland, J. L., and Gottfredson, G. D. "Student-College Congruency as a Predictor of Satisfaction." *Journal of Counseling Psychology*, 1975, *22*, 132–139.

Pace, C. R. *College and University Environment Scales Technical Manual*. 2nd. Ed. Princeton, N.J.: Educational Testing Service, 1969.

Pace, C. R., and Stern, G. G. "An Approach to the Measurement of Psychological Characteristics of College Environments." *Journal of Educational Psychology*, 1958, *49*, 269–277.

Painter, P., and Painter, N. "Placing Students for Stability and Success." In W. R. Lowery and Associates (Eds.), *College Admissions Counseling: A Handbook for the Profession*. San Francisco: Jossey-Bass, 1982.

Pavela, G. *The Dismissal of Students with Mental Disorders: Legal Issues, Policy Considerations, and Alternative Responses*. Asheville, N.C.: College Administration Publications, 1985.

Pervin, L. A. "A Twenty-College Study of Student-College Interaction Using TAPE (Transactional Analysis of Personality and Environment): Rationale, Reliability, and Validity." *Journal of Educational Psychology*, 1967, *58*, 290–302.

Peterson, R. E. *Technical Manual: College Student Questionnaire*, Ref. Ed. Princeton: Educational Testing Service, 1968.

Starr, A., Betz, E. L., and Menne, J. "Differences in College Student Satisfaction: Academic Dropouts, Nonacademic Dropouts, and Nondropouts." *Journal of Counseling Psychology*, 1972, *19*, 318–322.

Stern, G. G. *People in Context: Measuring Person-Environment Congruence in Education and Industry*. New York: Wiley, 1970.

Terenzini, P. T. "Designing Attrition Studies." In E. T. Pascarella (Ed.), *Studying Student Attrition*. New Directions for Institutional Research, no. 36. San Francisco: Jossey-Bass, 1982.

Walsh, W. B. *Theories of Person-Environment Interaction: Implications for the College Student*. Iowa City, Ia.: The American College Testing Program, 1973.

Walsh, W. B. "Some Theories of Person-Environment Interaction." *Journal of College Student Personnel*, 1975, *16*, 107–113.

Walsh, W. B. "Person-Environment Interaction." In J. H. Banning (Ed.), *Campus Ecology: A Perspective for Student Affairs.* Columbus, Oh.: National Association of Student Personnel Administrators, 1978.

Walsh, W. B., and Russell, J. H., III. "College Major Choice and Personal Adjustment." *Personnel and Guidance Journal,* 1969, *47,* 685–688.

Williams, T. E. "Recruiting Graduates: Understanding Student-Institution Fit." In D. R. Hossler (Ed.), *Enrollment Management: An Integrated Approach.* New York: The College Board, 1984.

Terry E. Williams is assistant professor and director, Graduate Programs in Higher Education, at Loyola University of Chicago.

Improving retention calls for methodical investigation and program design.

Assessing and Reducing Attrition

John P. Bean

Without students, there is no institution—no administration, no staff, no faculty —and yet student attrition has remained fairly constant at about 45 percent for the past century (Tinto, 1982). This represents a tremendous loss of talent and financial support for the institution. Three reasons to retain students are paramount: economic, ethical, and institutional.

The economic reason is most straightforward. There is a linear relationship between enrollment and income. If an institution has a break-even point of one thousand students, maintaining an enrollment of eleven hundred students represents an enormous cushion, since most classes can be 10 percent larger without additional cost to the institution. If the enrollment drops to nine hundred, however, the instructional costs remain the same, but faculty and other institutional employees may be faced with the loss of 10 percent of their income or 10 percent of their colleagues. Given a typical tuition of $5,000 at an institution enrolling eight hundred full-time freshmen where the freshman to sophomore year attrition rate is 25 percent, the loss of two hundred students would cost the school $1 million. Across the country, the tuition loss due to full-time freshman attrition alone would be $3 billion.

It is unethical to admit students for the benefit of the institution and not for the good of the student. Students must be informed of what will be required academically and socially to remain enrolled at an institution, and they need to know that "some college" does little to increase one's income above that of a high school graduate. A high attrition rate shows a failure on

D. Hossler (Ed.), *Managing College Enrollments*. New Directions for
Higher Education, no. 53. San Francisco: Jossey-Bass, March 1986.

the part of the institution to select or to socialize students to the academic and social values of the college or university. Admitting students who have academic and social characteristics appropriate for an institution may do more to reduce attrition than any postmatriculation program.

The third cost of attrition, the cost to the institutional fabric, is implied in the first two. A high attrition rate is likely to be associated with a low faculty morale. When faculty teach at an institution where attrition is high, they are likely to feel negative toward themselves and their profession. Attrition is ordinarily viewed as student failure, but institutions with high rates of attrition can also be viewed as failures, and the best students, faculty, staff, and administrators will try to leave.

Attrition is costly in terms of dollars, faculty morale and quality, and for ethical reasons. Before describing the attrition process and what can be done to counteract it, this chapter defines attrition and discusses the importance of understanding the factors affecting attrition at a particular institution.

There are a variety of issues to consider in developing retention programs, depending on the perspective from which attrition is seen. I use a definition of attrition from the institutional perspective. A dropout is a student who withdraws from an institution for one year or more and has not completed his or her formally declared program of study. Thus, a student who transfers to another school *is* a dropout, but the student who intends to take one or more courses and completes these courses without getting a degree is *not* a dropout. Dropout occurs when the student leaves an institution before reaching his or her educational objective. Thus, the dropout rate cannot be computed by comparing the sizes of the freshmen and sophomore classes.

A student who leaves for a year and then returns to school is considered a dropout because leaving is costly to a college or university. Students who change from full-time to part-time status, for example, who drop from fifteen semester credit hours one term to three the next, are not considered dropouts even though their action is costly to the institution. Thus, any definition of attrition is limited, and the rate of attrition will change depending on how attrition is defined.

Administrators emphasize reducing the dropout rate, but the emphasis is misplaced. The issue is not the percentage of the total student body that drops out, but the retention rate for various types of students. Just as in marketing, where it is important to segment the population of potential clients, it is important in retention programs to identify the dropout rates for the different segments of the student population. For instance, the overall dropout rate for a commuter university may be 50 percent, but if only 10 percent of the full-time students drop out, while 40 percent of the part-time students drop out, the attrition problem is much less serious than if the reverse were true. Thus, an institution should be concerned with the attrition rates for full-time students, part-time students, minority students, students employed full-time, students with dependents, men versus women, students over twenty-five years old, commuter students versus resident students, freshmen, sophomores, juniors, seniors, and other important segments of the student body.

To believe there is one best way to increase retention is to fail to grasp the complexity of the issue. Institutions differ in degree level, missions, and quality. The heterogeneity in student and institutional type indicates that a single model of student attrition will tend to work poorly in explaining the dropout process for individual students at particular institutions. It is necessary and desirable to identify the sets of factors that influence attrition decisions for as many subgroups at the institution as possible. The results of research studies for similar students at similar institutions should indicate that the same factors lead to attrition decisions.

Beyond differences in demographic characteristics of students and differences in the structural characteristic of institutions, there are numerous legitimate reasons for students to drop out of school. For one student, it is grades; for another, it is to be with a high school sweetheart; for others, it is a lack of friends on campus, a lack of loyalty to the institution, not fitting in with other students, a lack of money, not understanding rules and regulations, or feeling alienated by the rules they do understand. In previous studies, lists of variables affecting attrition have surpassed fifty, and any one of those variables may be the key reason a student drops out. The heterogeneity of the institutions and the students who attend them limits our abilities to predict attrition. The remainder of this chapter discusses what is known (or believed) to affect attrition decisions and what institutions can do to reduce attrition.

Retention Models: Guideposts to the Causes and Cures of Student Attrition

Retention models are similar in structure but differ in the variables assumed to affect attrition. It is useful to present a general retention model and then to discuss how each of the various sets of variables affects attrition and what can be done to reduce attrition. The metamodel is presented in Figure 1.

The model indicates that the process of attrition depends on the background characteristics of students let into the program. Students interact with the college bureaucratically or organizationnally, as well as academically and socially, while the environment represents a simultaneous force that could pull a student away from the school. Organizational, academic, and social interactions lead to attitudes that affect institutional fit and institutional commitment—both potent predictors of continued enrollment. These combined attitudes affect intent to leave and retention-attrition decisions directly. GPA, which is related to past academic performance and academic integration, should affect decisions to continue enrollment directly, as should the environmental variables.

Background Variables. The characteristics of students most likely to remain in school until graduation are well known. These are students who were academically successful in high school, ranked high in their classes, took college

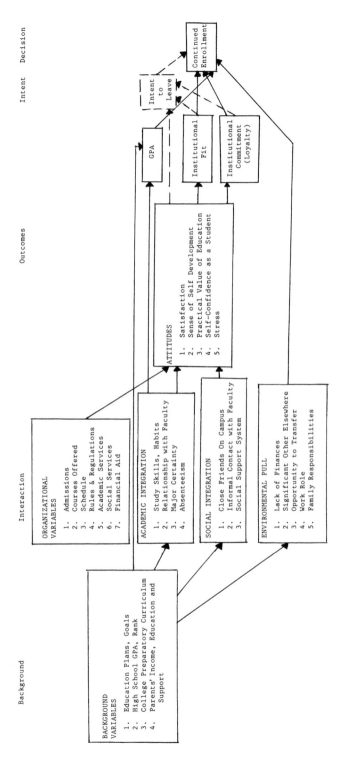

Figure 1. A Longitudinal Model of the Types of Factors Affecting Retention Decisions

Background   Interaction   Outcomes   Intent   Decision

BACKGROUND
VARIABLES
1. Education Plans, Goals
2. High School GPA, Rank
3. College Preparatory Curriculum
4. Parents' Income, Education and
   Support

ORGANIZATIONAL
VARIABLES
1. Admissions
2. Courses Offered
3. Schedule
4. Rules & Regulations
5. Academic Services
6. Social Services
7. Financial Aid

ACADEMIC INTEGRATION
1. Study Skills, Habits
2. Relationship with Faculty
3. Major Certainty
4. Absenteeism

SOCIAL INTEGRATION
1. Close Friends On Campus
2. Informal Contact with Faculty
3. Social Support System

ENVIRONMENTAL PULL
1. Lack of Finances
2. Significant Other Elsewhere
3. Opportunity to Transfer
4. Work Role
5. Family Responsibilities

ATTITUDES
1. Satisfaction
2. Sense of Self Development
3. Practical Value of Education
4. Self-Confidence as a Student
5. Stress

GPA

Institutional
Fit

Institutional
Commitment
(Loyalty)

Intent
to
Leave

Continued
Enrollment

preparatory courses, whose parents went to college and are well off financially and support their son or daughter's decision to attend college, and who have high but realistic educational goals. Elite institutions attract this kind of student and usually have the highest retention rates.

When taking background characteristics into account, an institution should engage in adaptive strategic planning (Cope, 1981). In brief, an institution needs to identify its strength and mission and then find students (resources in the environment) whose needs match the institution's strengths. Most institutions cannot compete at random for students but must attract specific types. In doing so, the institution can then provide the kinds of academic programs and support these students need in order to graduate. To cast a net too widely to attract a heterogenous student body means that a single retention program will help a small percentage of students, and an increasingly wider array of retention programs will be required.

The following activities related to background characteristics should enhance retention:

1. Identify the type of college or university you would like yours to be, and which it can be given your current resources.

2. Identify the type of student that is likely to succeed in such a college.

3. Reach out, by letter if not with college personnel, into the high schools that are current or potential sources of this kind of student and:

A. Encourage academic excellence in these high schools

B. Help develop policies that channel students with college potential into college preparatory curricula during their last three years of high school

C. Help develop career-planning workshops so that those students who will need a college education for their careers can take college preparatory courses and understand the linkage between the courses they take and their future work.

4. Do not ignore parents. Parental support has a major influence on how students in the traditional age group interact with their college environment. Students are more likely to remain enrolled if their parents understand college life and support the student's decision to attend college. Keeping parents informed of school requirements is a redundant mechanism for informing students about current requirements and activities. There should be an orientation to college for parents, ongoing on-campus programs for parents, and monthly newsletters. In the case of nontraditional students, spouses and employers should be given similar information.

Organizational Variables. It is among the organizational variables that retention and other student service programs should be placed in the model. Typically, single programs have little effect on the overall retention rate, either because only a small percentage of the student body takes advantage of such programs, or because those students who do may be selected into the program because they are most likely to drop out. Thus, participation in the program may be associated with high dropout rates. A variety of programs designed to meet the needs of different types of students, which provide meaningful involvement for students, staff, faculty, and administrators, and which focus on changing student attitudes, are most likely to increase retention.

The admissions office is the meeting point of the client (potential student) and the product (instruction). Admissions officers should be evaluated not by the number of students they enroll but by the number of students they enroll who come back to school as sophomores and who eventually graduate. Those who decide the criteria for admission shape the student body, and if done well, attrition should decline.

The courses offered, the times at which they are offered, and which ones and how many are required for graduation, also affect the retention rate. The curriculum itself probably has more to do with attrition than any other organizational factor. The types of academic and social services provided for students may also influence retention. Students may drop out if they feel a lack of academic support, such as academic advising, career counseling, instruction in the use of institutional resources (library, computer, and so on), study skill development programs, and basic or remedial work in particular content areas. In addition to these, co-curricular programs, such as debate or science clubs, theater and other special interest groups, residence life activities, intramural sports, and the student union programs and facilities, enhance the student's social integration into the institution and hence reduce attrition. Student health and counseling services are also organizational factors that can affect retention decisions.

The final organizational variable is financial aid. Students who do not have the funds necessary to pay for college are not (with only rare exceptions) allowed to attend college for free. If the institution is able to provide financial aid for these students by means of grants, loans, scholarships, or work-study programs, the institution alters the one-to-one correspondence between a failure to pay for school and involuntary withdrawal (dismissal). Although financial aid can help keep students enrolled, the research findings on the effect of financial aid on retention are mixed, since those with the least money often come from educationally disadvantaged families and attended lower-quality high schools.

The following organizational activities should enhance retention:

1. Admit students who match the institution's strengths. Find out what prospective students want from college and consider this information when making admissions decisions. Low morale due to a high dropout rate may make students who would otherwise stay more likely to leave. If you admit an underprepared student, provide the academic and social support the student needs in order to stay enrolled.

2. Offer the courses students want to take at times and places convenient to the student, not the faculty. An annual poll of students, their advisers, and potential students by admissions officers can identify unmet student course

needs. Putting the best instructors in introductory-level courses is both a good way to keep students enrolled in school and a device for recruiting departmental majors.

3. Use a zero-based budgeting approach to the rules and regulations governing student academic and social life: If there is insufficient reason to keep a rule, drop it. Students who feel controlled by rules and regulations become alienated and drop out of school—this is particularly true for minority students.

4. Provide meaningful academic support services. Students need advising, but institutions are sufficiently different so that no foolproof advising system exists. Advising is likely to reduce attrition when the advisers are concerned with and informed about the student seeking advice and are familiar with the options and regulations of the institution. Students who, with the help of their advisers, get a positive attitude toward themselves, their institution, and how their schooling fits in with their lives and careers are more likely to remain enrolled.

5. Provide a supportive social environment for students. Although this may not be a major concern for nontraditional students, it is a major concern for traditional ones. Students need the opportunity to develop friendships, interact with mentors, and have role models of how to behave as responsible students and productive members of society. Big-brother or big-sister programs, lounges, a student union, meeting places for intramural athletics and special interest groups, and advisers who are concerned with the students' academic and social development should enhance retention. The social environment is crucial in forming the attitudes associated with fitting into and staying enrolled in school.

Academic Integration. In order to succeed as a student, an individual needs both skills and attitudes appropriate for academic work. When a student develops proper attitudes toward integrity, delayed gratification, and valuing scholarship, the student is likely to perform well academically, which is manifest in a high or at least a rising GPA. Students who perform well are more likely to remain enrolled in a college or university, except for transfer students, who perform well in order to leave.

Study Skills and Habits. Few students are gifted enough to survive academic rigors without good study habits. Among these are time management skills, as well as skills in reading, writing, note-taking, preparing papers, and studying for exams. Programs that improve these skills are likely to enhance retention for students deficient in these areas.

Relationship with Faculty. There is a large body of literature indicating that informal contact with faculty members enhances academic integration and hence reduces attrition (Pascarella, 1980). Informal contact with faculty members who are concerned about students' cognitive and social development should result in positive attitudes toward school and should increase retention. At small schools where such contact is expected, it can reduce attrition due to its effect on positive attitudes toward oneself, clarification of career goals, and an increase in confidence in one's student role. At major research universities with large undergraduate student bodies, the faculty are often so involved in research and graduate teaching that informal contacts with freshman students are rare and hence have little effect on retention. Such contact would probably be beneficial, but it is unreasonable to assume that research-oriented faculty have the time for or interest in extensive personal contact with undergraduate students.

Certainty of Choice of Major. Students with a major have an identity and can share values and fit in with a particular social group. They also have direction and should be able to link course work with later employment. On the other hand, students who have little notion of which major to choose have a hard time seeing how the courses they take fit together into a cohesive whole. Forcing students into early decisions about their major may be unwise, but delaying too long creates problems with unmet requirements. Ongoing discussions with both faculty and staff advisers concerning academic focus should reduce attrition. By the end of the freshman year, a student should have a plan of study for completing college. This plan can be adjusted as necessary.

Absenteeism. Absenteeism is one of the first signs that a student is dissatisfied with school, is under stress, or is having difficulties with the coursework. However, the effects of absenteeism on attrition depend on a student's GPA. For students with high GPAs, absenteeism is not related to dropout (Bean, 1982). But students who are absent from class and who also have low GPAs should meet with an academic counselor or adviser to find out whether the student is considering dropping out and, if so, whether the institution can or should do anything to change the student's intention to leave school.

The following should help the student's academic integration into an institution and, hence, enhance retention:

1. The institution should identify entering students who are likely to need improved study skills to remain in school. Require these students to participate in academic assistance programs.

2. A course, entitled something like "University 101," should be given for credit and required of all students. The purpose of this course is to provide students with information about the campus and its services, to link students with special needs to special services, to explore career options, to answer questions about institutional rules and requirements, to provide informal contact with a faculty or staff member, to provide information about campus traditions, and to be a social support group for adjusting to life at college. A modification of this course might be required of nontraditional students. This becomes a method of institutionalizing informal or at least semiformal contacts with faculty members.

3. Groups of perhaps twenty students should be assigned to the same basic courses so that they get to know other students well.

4. Students should explore career options early in their schooling and should develop a program of study by the middle of their sophomore year.

5. Class attendance should be monitored. When absenteeism is high and grades are low, talk to the student and see if the institution can do anything to help.

Social Integration. Finding a social niche in which students share values and support each other through friendship and mutual concern for each other's well being is typically viewed as central to keeping students enrolled in school (Tinto, 1975). While there is good evidence for this view among traditional students, for nontraditional students, who have a peer group and social support outside of the institution and who may be older and have already formed a mature set of values, social integration probably plays a reduced role in enhancing retention decisions (Bean and Metzner, 1986).

Close Friends on Campus. Students who have close friendships on campus are likely to feel satisfied with being a student and feel that they fit in at school. Social events, living arrangements, and places where social groups can gather can foster the development of friendships. Special interest groups can also bring students together for social as well as academic support. Programs do not make friends, but an absence of programs may hamper friendships from developing.

Informal Contact with Faculty. Just as contact with faculty may increase academic integration, it may also affect social integration. Students who feel accepted by faculty members and consider faculty members as friends as well as mentors are more likely to stay enrolled in school. There is something of a chicken-egg problem here, however, because faculty members often select the brightest students to befriend. Nonetheless, such informal contact may be very meaningful for students if it can be fostered.

Social Support System. The important thing is that a student feels that someone on the campus cares about the student as a whole person, not just as a number or a source of tuition. Most social support probably comes from other students (for traditional students) because it is with each other that students have the most contact. However, support from family, friends, faculty, residence hall staff, counselors, staff members who process student forms, secretaries, custodians, central administrators, and alumni can all influence a student's attitudes toward a school.

The following should aid a student's social integration into an institution, improving the student's attitudes toward the school and sense of fitting in and, hence, retention:

1. Provide informal gathering places on campus. For example, place faculty mailboxes by departmental lounges, where students and faculty can meet by chance.

2. Have social events students want to attend. These will vary depending on the student body, but try to bring students together in an environment in which they are likely to converse.

3. Publicize extensively special interest groups, how to join them, and

what they do. Consider requiring membership in at least one out-of-class program during the student's second semester at school.

4. Get the whole campus involved in paying attention to the needs of students. Be a flexible bureaucracy when necessary and a collegium when possible.

5. Do not neglect parents. Keep them informed and indicate that their support is valuable for keeping their son or daughter enrolled.

Environmental Pull. Environmental factors are, by definition, things over which the institution has little control, but which contribute to decisions to remain in or drop out of school. It is important to recognize that eliminating all attrition is neither desirable nor possible. Institutional resources should not be wasted trying to change or control things over which the institution has no power. The four environmental factors listed here comprise only a partial list. Specific factors, such as a family crisis, serious health problems, or the closing of a local business, may result in students leaving school. It is of little use for a school to try to anticipate such events, but instead it should look at an attrition rate of perhaps 5 to 7 percent as a baseline.

There are five environmental variables that seem of major importance: Students who lack or perceive they lack finances are likely to withdraw from school. Students who want to be with a significant other elsewhere or who have an opportunity to transfer to another school are also likely to leave or transfer. Students, especially nontraditional students, who have work responsibilities or family responsibilities may leave school due to these outside responsibilities (see Bean and Metzner, 1986).

Although institutions can do little to counteract environmental variables, the retention rate may be improved by

- Not only providing as much financial aid as possible but communicating financial aid options to students and, when relevant, to parents, spouses, and employers
- Providing full-time work on campus for students when reasonable and appropriate
- Scheduling courses at times convenient for students who must work and providing safe transportation or parking facilities
- Providing child care for students with family responsibilities.

Attitudes and Other Outcomes. Students with positive attitudes toward their college or university are likely to remain enrolled in school. Students enroll with a set of attitudes toward the school that are modified by the student's experience at school. When a student arrives with positive attitudes toward the school and has positive organizational, academic, and social experiences, these positive attitudes are likely to be maintained or to increase. When the reverse is true, the student is likely to leave. Any program aimed at increasing retention should have as its first priority affecting a student's attitude toward self or school. This should not be done in a manipulative way, but the service or activity provided should be evaluated in terms of its impact on student attitudes, not just on how well the service was delivered or to how many students. A general sense of satisfaction, self-development, the practical value of an education for securing employment, and an increased sense of self-confidence as a student are a core block of attitudes affecting retention. Excessive stress, in contrast, reduces the likelihood of a student remaining enrolled.

Institutional fit and institutional commitment are the specific attitudes toward the institution that closely affect the decision to remain enrolled in school. These attitudes must be nurtured if a student is to remain enrolled. Attitudes toward the self and the institution are based on the more general attitudes and experiences a student has had in school.

College GPA is affected primarily by high school GPA. Students who do well academically in high school are likely to do well in college. However, academic integration has direct and substantial effects on college GPA, so the institution bears some responsibility for providing both the environment and the services needed to develop students academically.

Intent to leave is included in the model because intentions are hypothesized to intervene between attitudes and behavior (Fishbein and Ajzen, 1975). The variable is content free, however, and is not an explanation of why students decide to stay or leave. The variable is valuable as a predictor of retention. Students who intend to leave are least likely to stay enrolled, and by asking students if they intend to return to school for the next semester or year, institutions can identify very simply those students who are at the highest risk of dropping out. After identifying these students we can query them as to why they intend to leave. When ethical and appropriate, programs can be provided that increase the likelihood of the student remaining in school.

Conducting Retention Studies

There are a large number of factors that can affect retention decisions, and the relative importance of each factor differs at different schools and for different types of students. It is a great advantage to an institution to conduct a study identifying factors affecting continued enrollment decisions.

There are two general approaches to studying student retention. The first is to use data that in many instances already exist to describe students who remain in or drop out of school. These can be described in terms of demographic characteristics (age, sex, ethnicity, high school attended) and previous academic characteristics (high school grades, college preparatory courses, standardized test scores), as well as current student's information (enrollment information, major, residence, class level). The student body can then be disaggregated and the rates of attrition calculated for each sizable group of students. In addition, the time at which attrition occurs can also be identified (for example, after one semester or between the sophomore and junior years). In this way the institution can identify who is dropping out and when. However, little information can be gathered about why a student is dropping out.

The second type of study is analytical and requires gathering information from individual students rather than from student records. Three methods for gathering data are common: "autopsy," or post hoc (after the student has dropped out); cross sectional, when questionnaire data are gathered only once; and longitudinal, when information is gathered from students more than once.

Autopsy studies are easy to interpret but may lead to erroneous conclusions. People tend to rationalize past behavior in normatively acceptable ways. Thus, students commonly report that they left school due to inadequate finances because that is a socially acceptable reason, when in fact they could have found additional financial resources. Autopsy studies also lead to erroneous conclusions because no control group is used. Dropouts might indicate that they left school due to poor advising, but a survey of students still enrolled might find the same low appraisal of advising. So advising may not be related to continued enrollment, despite the findings from the autopsy study.

Cross-sectional studies have the advantage of including students who both drop out of and stay in school. A survey is taken of students before completing a semester or a year, and these students are tracked to see if they return to school. After these enrollment data are collected, they can be analyzed in a univariate mode, using analysis of variance to find if there are significant differences on variables between dropouts and persisters. The data can also be used in more sophisticated multivariate analyses, such as path analysis, to better explain the dropout process. Such an approach requires a social science researcher familiar with sampling, questionnaire construction and administration, data entry, and computer analyses using multivariate statistics. Such a procedure costs more but provides substantially better insights into the process of retention and attrition than demographic or autopsy studies.

The third type of study is longitudinal and involves gathering data from students at more than one time. Similar to cross-sectional studies, the analysis of the data can become very complex, but again, this type of study increases one's understanding of the attrition process. For example, longitudinal studies can identify how attitudes change over time and how the factors affecting retention change. There is one additional problem with this type of study, that of sample decay. With each successive round of data collection, the sample for which complete data is available becomes smaller and therefore less representative of the entire population. Despite this limitation, this type of study may give a more accurate picture of the attrition process than the others.

Although data for cross-sectional and longitudinal studies are often collected with paper and pencil questionnaires, naturalistic, ethnographic, and interview techniques can provide a richer set of data to be analyzed. Again, a researcher familiar with these methods would be needed to conduct such a study.

I would encourage concerned institutions to at least complete a descriptive study to identify the size of their attrition problem and the types of students they retain or lose. With more resources, a cross-sectional paper and pencil survey is recommended. Intent to leave can be substituted for actual attrition data, and the analysis can be made as soon as the data are collected. From an administrative cost-benefit approach, this type of study provides the best information about attrition within reasonable time limits and at a reasonable cost. Longitudinal studies are probably best for theory development and give the greatest insight into retention-attrition decisions but may continue for years and cost substantially more than other types of research. Those interested in conducting research on attrition should refer to *Studying Student Attrition,* (Pascarella, 1982).

Evaluation of Retention Programs

I do not wish to describe a detailed process for evaluating retention programs. I feel central administrators who expect a retention office, by some magic, to reduce the attrition rate from 30 percent to 25 percent, have missed the point. Outcome evaluation works well when all those accountable for an outcome are the ones responsible for producing the outcome. In this case, any employees of the college or university can influence the rate of attrition. To assume that attrition is the responsibility of a student services office ignores the roles of faculty, staff, and other students in affecting retention.

Those wishing to know if retention efforts are fruitful should not simply look at the bottom line. As coaches often say, if you play the game well, the score will take care of itself. The most effective retention program that can be developed is one that results in the school clearly identifying a mission about which there is a consensus on campus, admitting students suited to its mission, and changing the attitudes of staff, faculty, administrators, and other employees and upper division students so that lower-division students (where attrition rates are highest) develop positive academic skills and attitudes about the schools. If the attrition rate stays high regardless of this effective program, it is probably due to environmental factors.

Conclusion

This chapter has described the process of student attrition and provided an explanation of why certain programs should reduce attrition. In this way readers can decide for themselves, based on the types of students enrolled at their institution, their institutional resources, and their institution's missions, which of the many possible retention programs would likely be most effective in reducing attrition.

In addition to the ideas for increasing student retention that I mentioned earlier, the following are some other general ideas associated with successful retention programs.

1. The effort should be unified, not fragmented. The central administration and the faculty must endorse the program and actively participate in retention efforts. The program cannot consist of only student affairs staff.

2. Make an effort to change students' attitudes, not merely a single behavior.

3. Identify different types of students and tailor programs to their specific needs. While serving these perceived needs, staff members should refer students to other support systems.

4. Use strategic planning and market the college. Attract students that are appropriate for the product the college offers. Identify competitors. Offer something special. Do not try to attract everybody.

5. Identify exit-prone students early. Find out why they intend to leave. Provide a needed service when appropriate.

6. Prolong orientation. Give special help to students who are the first in their family to attend college. Provide special orientation for students' parents, transfer students, nontraditional students (that is, those who are not in the majority at the school).

7. Use committed advisers and provide them with information about the individuals they advise, so that they do not simply hand students one brochure for required courses and another for choice of majors.

8. Provide a social support system for students (involving parents, spouses, peers, big brothers or big sisters, social gatherings, car pools, cocurricular activities, residence hall programs, and so on). During the first year, groups of the same students should be in the same classes. Develop a caring attitude on campus. Help the student fit in.

9. Provide an academic support system, but remember, recruiting will probably affect grades more than on-campus programs. When on-campus remedial programs are necessary, make them fun and attractive.

10. Have the faculty take time to explain how the skills (communication, quantitative, analytical) learned in courses are valued by employers. Orient students to the advantages of a college degree.

11. Create and use symbols and rituals to promote the image of the school. Teach the student why graduating from your institution is something special. Believe it yourself. Create the intangible atmosphere that makes a student ever loyal.

12. Turn your best graduates into recruiters. Turn your richest graduates into supporters.

References

Bean, J. P. "The Interaction Effects of GPA on Other Determinants of Student Attrition in a Homogeneous Population." Paper presented at the annual meeting of the American Educational Research Association, New York, April 1982.

Bean, J. P., and Metzner, B. S. "A Conceptual Study of Nontraditional Undergraduate Student Attrition." *Review of Educational Research*, 1986, *55* (4), 485–540.

Cope, R. G. *Strategic Planning, Management, and Decision-Making.* AAHE-ERIC/Higher Education Research Report no. 9. Washington, D.C.: American Association for Higher Education, 1981.

Fishbein, M. and Ajzen, I. *Belief, Attitude, Intention, and Behavior: An Introduction to Theory and Research.* Reading, Mass.: Addison Wesley, 1975.

Pascarella, E. T. "Student-Faculty Informal Contact and College Outcomes." *Review of Educational Research*, 1980, *50* (4), 545–595.

Pascarella, E. T. (ed.). *Studying Student Attrition.* New Directions for Institutional Research, no. 36. San Francisco: Jossey-Bass, 1982.

Tinto, V. "Dropout from Higher Education: A Theoretical Synthesis of Recent Research." *Review of Educational Research*, 1975, *45* (1), 89–125.

Tinto, V. "Defining Dropout: A Matter of Perspective." In Pascarella, E. T. (ed.). *Studying Student Attrition.* New Directions for Institutional Research, no. 36. San Francisco: Jossey-Bass, 1982.

John P. Bean is assistant professor of higher education at Indiana University, Bloomington.

*The renewed interest in monitoring students' educational
progress suggests that marketing college outcomes may become an
indispensible component of a comprehensive enrollment
management strategy.*

Outcomes-Oriented Marketing

*George D. Kuh
George H. Wallman*

Prospective college students, particularly those with outstanding high school
records and test scores, are bombarded with promotional material and often
receive telephone calls or visits from college admissions officers. In response
to a declining pool of high school graduates, some institutions have resorted
to hard-sell techniques, including misleading statements about their institutions
(Walters, 1982).

With a shrinking demand for college education, the full-service institution that attempts to provide everything any student wants or needs ''does not
make economic sense'' (Kotler, 1976, p. 59). According to Zemsky and Oedel
(1983) institutional viability depends more on quality than on quantity; that
is, the perceived value of the educational process is more important than the
number of students enrolled in an institution of higher education (IHE). In
a saturated market, an IHE is more likely to achieve efficiency and a salient
market position through a clearer, more specialized delineation of how it differs from others (Zemsky and Oedel, 1983). One way to become distinctive
within an IHE market segment is through documenting institution-specific
benefits of attendance (Kuh and others, 1984; Litten and others, 1983). Although there is general agreement that the benefits of college should be communicated more broadly, admissions officers surprisingly have not considered
familiarity with the outcomes of college attendance to be particularly important

D. Hossler (Ed.), *Managing College Enrollments.* New Directions for
Higher Education, no. 53. San Francisco: Jossey-Bass, March 1986.

to their work (Spaight and Sperry, 1980). Fueled by renewed interest in the quality of public schooling, the attention currently focused on value-added assessments of students' progress in college (Astin, 1985) may prompt more widespread use of college outcomes information by institutional advancement officers.

The purposes of this chapter are twofold: first, to summarize the outcomes of college attendance that enhance the attractiveness of the option of postsecondary education to prospective students; and second, to provide some examples of institution-specific outcomes that an IHE can use to differentiate its market segment position and enhance its attractiveness to students within that market. Competing interpretations of the concept of college outcomes are briefly reviewed, and the purposes for using information about the benefits of college attendance are discussed. Then, the general outcomes of college are summarized. Finally, suggestions are offered for using institution-specific benefits in an enrollment management strategy.

What Is an Outcome of College?

The influence of college on students has been described in several ways. In the "pipeline" analogy, characteristics of students (for example, high school rank, SAT scores, socioeconomic status) are considered preordinate in that if an IHE attracts bright, able, highly motivated students, graduates will be bright, able, highly motivated, and probably attain responsible, productive positions in society. In that interpretation, the institution itself has little impact; whatever benefits that accrue to graduates are primarily a function of students' characteristics, often described as "inputs" (Astin, 1974; Kuh, 1981). In the "factory" analogy, the college is thought to be an imprinting experience because an institution's resources (faculty, facilities, peer group) exert a definitive influence on students' intellectual and social behavior; graduates hold similar world views and values and are uniquely equipped for service to society. In this interpretation, an IHE takes in raw materials (students' characteristics) and molds the student into an educated person who is qualitatively "different" from graduates of other institutions.

A more realistic analogy to what takes place during college may be the fitness center. Membership in a fitness center does not guarantee physical or psychological well-being. Unless an individual uses the facility to exercise regularly, physical fitness benefits will not accrue. Similarly, the benefits to be derived from attending college vary depending on the degree to which students take advantage of the institution's resources. That is, differentiated outcomes associated with college attendance are a function of the interaction between students and the institution's resources mediated by the degree to which students expend effort in interacting with institutional agents and peers (Astin, 1985; Kuh, 1981; Pace, 1980). In addition, "the level of students' involvement in college activities seems to be a critical factor in distinguishing between satisfied, high-achieving students and those who are less well integrated to the academic and social life of the institution" (Kuh, 1985, p. 4).

For the purposes of this chapter, an outcome of college is any intended or unintended product or effect of the interaction between a student's characteristics (intellectual ability, aspirations, and socioeconomic status), institutional resources (size of student body, quality of faculty and staff, facilities) and the degree to which the student is involved in curricular and extracurricular learning activities (Kuh, 1981). Outcomes can be identified using indices of intellectual or emotional development, achievement measures such as grades or leadership positions, vocational skills, and alumni attainments such as income and participation in community service activities. In general, more powerful indices are those that demonstrate "value added" or positive changes or gains between assessments made at the beginning of college and at the end of or after college (Astin, 1980).

General Outcomes of College

Comprehensive syntheses of the variety of benefits associated with college attendance have been prepared by Bowen (1977), Feldman and Newcomb (1969), and Pace (1979). Those desiring a fuller treatment of the general outcomes of college are encouraged to consult one or more of these presentations.

The general benefits of college can be distilled into four categories: knowledge and intellectual development, social development, personal development, and career and vocational development (Kuh, 1985).

Knowledge and Intellectual Development. In general, the relationship between knowledge and education is linear; the higher the levels of college completed, the more one knows. However, college grades are not powerful predictors of postcollege accomplishments. The relationship between grades and out-of-class involvement in the academic and social life of an institution seems to be curvilinear in that students who participate at moderate levels in extracurricular activities seem to perform better academically.

College attendance is also related to gains in measures of intellectual development such as critical thinking, thinking introversion, cognitive complexity, and reflective judgement. Intellectual development exhibited by students between matriculation and graduation is usually greater than that of cohorts who do not attend college (Trent and Medsker, 1968), and these differences seem to persist into the adult years. Among the most frequently cited (by alumni) lasting effects of college are the increased capacity for verbal and written expression and the ability to think clearly. Gains on measures of intellectual development may be greater for students at very selective small liberal arts colleges; however, this conclusion is tempered by findings that suggest that such differences generally "are much more closely linked to variation in ability that existed prior to the student's entrance to college than *any* characteristic of the undergraduate's institutions" (Astin and Panos, 1969, p. 145).

Social Development. College attendance is related to the liberalization of attitudes, political and social sophistication, increased confidence and competence in working with others, increased tolerance of persons different from oneself, and decreased dogmatism and ethnocentrism. Compared to those who have not gone to college, college graduates are more involved in civic activities, more likely to vote, more aware of political affairs, and are more involved in community service activities. According to Pace (1974, p. 129), "the attainment of a broad range of personal and social benefits . . . seems to be related to the extent to which the college experience itself provided a rich opportunity for personal and social relationships, involvement in campus activities, and in associations with faculty."

Personal Development. College students become more introspective, more appreciative of the esthetic qualities of life, more aware of their emotions, interests, values, and aspirations, more self-assured and self-sufficient, and less anxious. They also increase in the capacity to take interpersonal risks and to develop meaningful, lasting relationships. While interest and participation in formal religious practices typically decrease during college, many alumni become involved again in religious observances some years after graduation and are more likely to participate in religious activities than those who have not gone to college (Bowen, 1977).

Career and Vocational Development. Most college graduates (between two-thirds and three-quarters) obtain employment in the fields that are related to their major fields of study in college. Several years after college, between 80 and 90 percent of male graduates have relatively high-status occupations in that they are employed at the two highest occupational levels, professional and managerial. College graduates are less likely to be laid off, are paid more per hour, and work more hours in any given year than nongraduates. In addition, some evidence exists to suggest that college graduates tend to be more efficient consumers than nongraduates (Michael, 1975).

The rate of return on a college investment declined from 10–15 percent in the early 1960s to about 7.5 percent in the late 1970s. But recent evidence indicates that the earnings differential between high school and college graduates is increasing once again (Freeman, 1982). If nonmonetary benefits (such as job satisfaction, service to society, and quality of life), are considered, the rate of return on college investment may exceed 22 percent, about three times the average cost. While occupational status does not appear to be related to the quality of an institution attended (Alwin, 1976; Trusheim and Crouse, 1981), the quality of the institution may be related to postcollege income (Solmon, 1973; Wachtel, 1975). The earnings difference may be linked to the status of the firm or corporation one joins after graduation (firms pay more to attract graduates from prestigious IHEs).

Institution-Specific Outcomes Information

While college attendance rates are influenced by certain economic forces, such as the availability of jobs for high school graduates and rate of return on investment in college, the proportion of high school graduates going on to college in some states differs markedly from the national average of 53 percent. For example, in North Dakota, nearly 70 percent of the high school graduates go on to some form of postsecondary education, compared with less than 40 percent in Indiana. In areas with low college attendance rates, marketing strategies should emphasize information that describes the general advantages of attending college (such as postcollege income). In areas with high college attendance rates, colleges must disseminate information that describes superior programs and documents the quality of their institution relative to others in their market segment (Zemsky and Oedel, 1983).

In the process of converting interest in a variety of colleges to choosing one among several institutions, information about student satisfaction with the institution, interaction with peers and faculty, proportion of students holding leadership positions in extracurricular and academic organizations (Kuh and others, 1984), and number of graduates employed by prestigious law or accounting firms can be persuasive when shared with prospective students. Institution-specific outcomes information is most useful after a prospective student has selected a particular market segment; for example, private institutions versus public institutions or in-state versus out-of-state institutions (Zemsky and Oedel, 1983).

Prospective students and their parents are influenced by the status of vocational outcomes such as the positions obtained by graduates and the number of graduates from an institution who go on law school or medical school, compared with graduates from other institutions (Litten and Brodigan, 1982). While the validity of such comparisons may be specious (Krukowski, 1985), what happens to a college's graduates does influence how the institution is perceived. At North Dakota State University, this kind of information has been integrated into a comprehensive marketing strategy that has struck a responsive chord in prospective students, as the institution has experienced a 52 percent increase in enrollment since the implementation of an outcomes-oriented marketing plan in 1975.

Admissions Publications. Most IHEs rely primarily on printed material to make prospective students aware of academic programs and procedures. Publications seem to be an effective medium when communicating facts about the institution (Litten and Brodigan, 1982). Other information, such as quality of teaching or campus social climate, is considered valuable by prospective students and parents if this information comes from what are perceived to be reliable sources (such as the high school counselor or current students).

In the early 1970s, North Dakota State University (NDSU) revised its printed materials and instituted a series of "fact sheets," an informative, inexpensive, easily updated way of responding to three common questions asked by most prospective students: What kind of courses will I take? What kinds of jobs are available on completion of a specific degree program? What have been the attainments of graduates from this program?

Academic departments have provided illustrative programs of study, information about career options available to their majors, and the names of successsful alumni. For example, the Department of Agricultural Engineering fact sheet indicates that four hundred students have completed this program in the past ten years, one of the highest number in the nation, and that graduates hold well-paying positions as professional engineers, college professors, and development engineers for farm equipment manufacturing firms. The proportions of graduates from the agricultural engineering program obtaining positions in various fields are also provided; for example, soil and water engineering —15 percent; farm power and machinery—35 percent; farm structures—15 percent; electric power and processing—15 percent; farming—15 percent; and other—5 percent.

The Chemistry Department is noted for a program of study in polymers and coatings. The departmental fact sheet provides a history of the department and underscores its worldwide reputation, the credentials of its faculty, and information about the demand for graduates. The fact sheet also identifies the nation's major coatings companies in which polymers and coatings alumni hold professional and managerial positions. This information is very attractive to students concerned about postgraduation employment.

The fact sheet for the Construction Management Department in the College of Engineering and Architecture explains that summer employment opportunities are available for construction management students through the North Dakota Association of General Contractors. Many construction management graduates are employed by companies for which they served as summer interns during college.

NDSU has over one hundred fact sheets covering all academic programs. Fact sheets are preprinted with a heading, and final copy is produced on an 8½-by-11-inch sheet using a rapid printing service. While academic departments are responsible for providing basic subject matter, an admissions staff member assists with copyediting. Notebooks containing all of the available fact sheets are assembled and mailed to all high school and community college counselors in the university's two-state region (Litten and Brodigan, 1982).

The fact sheet is only one element of a comprehensive marketing strategy in which outcomes data are used. In an effort to reverse a substantial enrollment decline, the newly appointed dean of the College of Engineering and Architecture committed the college in 1975 to a comprehensive marketing program integrated with the institution's overall marketing strategy. Before providing copy for publications and letters for direct mailing efforts, the dean and his staff collected information about the postcollege accomplishments of alumni. The results of their data gathering indicated that many of the college's graduates were employed by some of the best and largest engineering and architecture firms in the United States, and all written materials for the marketing program contained information about the impressive attainments of the college's graduates. In the eight years following the initiation of the marketing strategy, the college experienced a fourfold increase in students; anecdotal information indicated that sharing information about graduates' career and vocational development had been important to the success of this marketing effort.

Alumni Publications. Publications directed to alumni are another vehicle for disseminating information about the outcomes associated with attendance at a particular college; these publications are often read by alumni or friends of the college who share this information with prospective students, thus expanding the applicant pool.

The NDSU alumni newspaper often contains articles describing the impressive accomplishments of alumni. Issues are mailed to prospective students and made available to students and parents visiting the campus. Inserts to alumni publications are designed specifically for prospective students and highlight particularly successful alumni. This information is of interest both to alumni and to prospective students, and it can be mailed as part of the alumni publication or used for independent periodic mailings to prospective students.

A recent issue of the NDSU alumni newspaper contains profiles of six students who participated in the university's Cooperative Education Program and subsequently received full-time job offers from the companies with which they had held internships. Another issue contains interviews summarizing currently enrolled students' perceptions of the NDSU faculty, facilities, and their experiences in class. This issue was presented as a surrogate measure of student satisfaction with the institution.

Several of NDSU's academic units produce newsletters for their own alumni. The College of Home Economics (CHE) featured stories of recent graduates who started successful small businesses in interior design, nutrition counseling, and bridal gown manufacturing. These issues were sent to all prospective students who indicated an interest in home economics as a major. Addressing the question of what students can do with a home economics degree, a special issue of the *CHE Newsletter* contained numerous profiles of graduates with successful careers in fields directly related to their degree work. The College of Science and Mathematics produces a similar newsletter.

Information documenting career and vocational development and attainments of graduates substantiates claims about a college or department's enviable reputation, and it provides specific information that responds to questions from prospective students and their parents about the link between attending a particular college and success after graduation.

Intellectual and Personal Growth Outcomes Information

A rich literature exists describing development during the college years (Astin, 1977; Chickering, 1969), but, for college marketing purposes, there is a paucity of information available about using data documenting students' achievements both in and out of the classroom. As institutional researchers become more familiar with instruments designed to assess value-added contributions related to college attendance (Forrest and Steele, 1982; Mentokowski and Doherty, 1984), more campus-specific data describing changes in students' intellectual and social-emotional functioning will become available. This information can be aggregated in various ways (for example, major, year of study, home town, high school attended) and communicated to prospective students through fact sheets, alumni publications, and other marketing vehicles.

Parents, particularly those who have attended college, are interested in nonpecuniary benefits of college, such as enhancement of interpersonal skills and deepening of values (Litten and Brodigan, 1982). College admissions personnel can use information about personal and social development outcomes to prepare prospective students and parents for the challenges to attitudes and values coterminous with the first few months of college attendance. Many students encounter difficulty in managing emotions and dealing with the autonomy and independence common to the first year of college. When talking with students in the final stages of selecting a college, admissions personnel should describe the support services available to assist students grappling with these challenges. Knowledge about traditional-age students' growth and development and desired outcomes in these domains can help an admissions counselor better understand and appreciate the behavior and aspirations of students with whom they come into contact.

This kind of information is presented during the training program for new NDSU admissions personnel, and staff are challenged to invent ways of incorporating this information about desired outcomes in the marketing strategy and during visits with students and parents. When appropriate, admissions staff attempt to use this information to make students aware of ''desired'' outcomes.

Also at NDSU, the *Student Development Task Inventory* (Winston and others, 1979) is used to familiarize parents with the developmental challenges students typically encounter during the first year of college. This information helps parents anticipate their children becoming more autonomous, developing a clearer sense of purpose in life, and establishing deeper, more meaningful interpersonal relationships. Response to this presentation has been very positive, as parents welcome information about dimensions of personal growth that are easily understood but often overlooked. In a sense, the presentation gives parents permission to consider the college years as a potentially developmentally powerful period in their child's life, and not only a route to a decent job and lifestyle after graduation. Similar information is shared with students during fall orientation and supports the developmental programming efforts implemented through the departments of residential life and student activities as well as in the classroom.

Prospective students are also encouraged to complete the *Self-Directed Search* (Holland, 1971). This self-administered vocational inventory correlates personality characteristics with the characteristics of work environments. Since a satisfying, challenging job is considered an important outcome of college (Krukowski, 1985), this exercise provides an opportunity for the prospective student and parents to discuss career goals and desired outcomes with an admissions officer.

Value-added assessments in the intellectual and personal growth domains have considerable potential for use in marketing IHEs. Numerous measurement problems are associated with efforts to monitor student progress during college, however (Feldman and Newcomb, 1969). Institutional advancement officers are encouraged to consult with measurement experts on their campus and remain current with the expanding literature on ways to document "value-added" outcomes of college.

Conclusion

College and university advancement officers rely too heavily on the public's tacit knowledge about the numerous and generally positive benefits of college. Communicating what is known about the benefits of college attendance with a higher level of specificity should work to the advantage of all IHEs. Printed material must be tailored for particular market segments (such as parents of college-bound students, students undecided about postsecondary education). Discovering what happens to students at a particular college can enhance an institution's position in its market segment. Given the increased interest in monitoring students' progress in college, communicating the outcomes associated with college attendance can become a marketing advantage for some institutions. Some years from now, it is possible that information documenting benefits related to college attendance will be routinely requested by all discerning applicants and potential donors.

References

Alwin, D. F. "Socioeconomic Background, Colleges, and Postcollege Achievements." In W. Sewell, R. Hauser, and D. Featherman (Eds.), *Schooling and Achievement in American Society.* New York: Academic Press, 1976.

Astin, A. W. "Measuring the Outcomes of Higher Education." In H. Bowen (Ed.), *Evaluating Institutions for Accountability.* New Directions for Institutional Research, no. 1. San Francisco: Jossey-Bass, 1974.

Astin, A. W. *Four Critical Years: Effects of College on Belief, Attitudes, and Knowledge.* San Francisco: Jossey-Bass, 1977.

Astin, A. W. "When Does a College Deserve to be Called 'High Quality?'" In *Improving Teaching and Institutional Quality.* 1980 Current Issues in Higher Education, no. 1. Washington, D.C.: American Association for Higher Education, 1980.

Astin, A. W. *Achieving Educational Excellence: A Critical Assessment of Priorities and Practices in Higher Education.* San Francisco: Jossey-Bass, 1985.

Astin, A. W., and Panos, R. J. *The Educational and Vocational Development of College Students.* Washington, D.C.: American Council on Education, 1969.

Bowen, H. R. *Investment in Learning: The Individual and Social Value of American Higher Education.* San Francisco: Jossey-Bass, 1977.

Chickering, A. W. *Education and Identity.* San Francisco: Jossey-Bass, 1969.

Feldman, K. A., and Newcomb, T. M. *The Impact of College on Students.* Vol. 1. San Francisco: Jossey-Bass, 1969.

Forrest, A., and Steele, J. M. *Defining and Measuring General Education Knowledge and Skills: Technical Report, 1976–81.* Iowa City, Ia.: American College Testing Program, 1982.

Freeman, R. B. *The Overeducated American in the 1980s.* Washington, D.C.: National Commission on Student Financial Assistance, 1982.

72

Holland, J. L. *Self-Directed Search*. Palo Alto, Calif.: Consulting Psychologists Press, 1971.

Kotler, P. "Applying Marketing Theory to College Admissions." In College Entrance Examination Board (Ed.), *A Role for Marketing in College Admissions*. New York: College Entrance Examination Board, 1976.

Krukowski, J. "What Do Students Want? Status." *Change*, 1985, *17* (3), 21-28.

Kuh, G. D. *Indices of Quality in the Undergraduate Experience*. AAHE-ERIC/Higher Education Research Report no. 4. Washington, D.C.: American Association for Higher Education, 1981.

Kuh, G. D. "The Case for Attendance: The Outcomes of Higher Education." *Journal of the National Association of College Admissions Counselors*, 1985, *107*, 3-9.

Kuh, G. D., Coomes, M. D. and Lundquist, I. A. "What Prospective Students Really Need to Know About Institutional Quality." *College and University*, 1984, *59*, 167-175.

Litten, L. H., and Brodigan, D. L. "On Being Heard in a Noisy World: Matching Messages and Media in College Marketing." *College and University*, 1982, *57*, 242-264.

Litten, L. H., Sullivan, D., and Brodigan, D. L. *Applying Market Research in College Admissions*. New York: College Entrance Examination Board, 1983.

Mentokowski, M., and Doherty, A. *Careering After College: Establishing the Validities of Abilities Learned in College for Later Careering and Professional Performance*. Milwaukee: Alverno College, 1984.

Michael, R. T. "Education and Fertility." In F. Juster (Ed.), *Education, Income, and Human Behavior*. New York: McGraw-Hill, 1975.

Pace, C. R. *The Demise of Diversity*. Berkeley, Calif.: Carnegie Commission on Higher Education, 1974.

Pace, C. R. *Measuring Outcomes of College: Fifty Years of Findings and Recommendations for the Future*. San Francisco: Jossey-Bass, 1979.

Pace, C. R. "Measuring the Quality of Student Effort." In *Improving Teaching and Institutional Quality*. 1980 Current Issues in Higher Education, no. 1. Washington, D.C.: American Association for Higher Education, 1980.

Solmon, L. C. "Schooling and Subsequent Success." In L. Solmon and P. Taubman (Eds.), *Does College Matter? Some Evidence on the Impacts of Higher Education*. New York: Academic Presss, 1973.

Spaight, E., and Sperry, R. E. "Employment, Training, and Evaluation of Admissions Personnel." *College and University*, 1980, *56* (1), 42-52.

Trent, J. W., and Medsker, L. L. *Beyond High School: A Psychosociological Study of 10,000 High School Graduates*. San Francisco: Jossey-Bass, 1968.

Trusheim, D., and Crouse, J. "Effects of College Prestige on Men's Occupational Status and Income." *Research in Higher Education*, 1981, *14* (4), 283-304.

Wachtel, P. "The Returns on Investment in Higher Education: Another View." In F. Juster (Ed.), *Education, Income, and Human Behavior*. New York: McGraw-Hill, 1975.

Walters, J. C. "Marketing Higher Education: Research, Planning, and Promotion." In W. R. Lowery and Associates (Eds.), *College Admissions Counseling: A Handbook for the Profession*. San Francisco: Jossey-Bass, 1982.

Winston, R., Miller, T. K., and Prince, J. S. *Student Development Task Inventory 2*. Athens, Ga.: Student Development Associates, 1979.

Zemsky, R., and Oedel, P. *The Structure of College Choice*. New York: College Entrance Examination Board, 1983.

George D. Kuh is professor and associate dean for academic affairs in the School of Education at Indiana University.

George H. Wallman is associate dean for student affairs and director of admissions and high school relations at North Dakota State University.

The skills of the institutional research office can be used to find out what actually happens between potential students' first show of interest and their enrollment, and why.

Using the Institutional Research Office

David L. Davis-Van Atta
Sam C. Carrier

Can institutional research be used profitably by an enrollment management program? Can academic market research and retention research aid the effectiveness of the enrollment management function? The answer to both of these questions is yes, because knowledge is power; information enables influence. The more one know about any process, the more likely one is to control it effectively. This chapter assumes general agreement with this basic principle. Institutional research, then, should have as its main goal in the enrollment management program simply this—to provide the information and understanding necessary to influence the processes controlling both the number and characteristics of the enrolled student body. Successful enrollment management, from this perspective, can thus be seen as the effective control of a set of distinct but interrelated processes. Research into the nature of these processes and the development of accurate models can provide the knowledge that enables such control.

Enrollment management involves, among other activities, establishing and meeting a numerical enrollment target while maintaining a student body congruent with the institution's mission. Enrollment management objectives are determined, optimally, at the highest levels of policy making within the college or university. They are realized through the coordination of highly varied

D. Hossler (Ed.), *Managing College Enrollments*. New Directions for Higher Education, no. 53. San Francisco: Jossey-Bass, March 1986.

activities by diverse groups, activities that often cut across organizational lines. Enrollment management is necessarily a team effort. We assume that the institution has some means of establishing, monitoring, and reviewing the enrollment target and the institution's mission, as well as assessing the effectiveness of the enrollment management program in meeting its objectives. We will therefore focus on the role institutional research plays in the enrollment management team.

Enrollment management in higher education is not afforded the luxury of time. The demographic decline that began in the late 1970s has already had an impact on higher education; the impact will almost certainly increase into the 1990s. It is doubtful that those responsible for their institution's enrollment would wish professional success or failure to be sustained purely by intuition, however well that intuition is tempered by experience. To be successful, we must gain a sound understanding of the individuals involved in making decisions about college choice and persistence, and we must understand the forces that consciously or unconsciously influence them. This knowledge will enable us to exert systematic, reasoned influence over the processes controlling enrollment so as to maximize desired ends such as the size of that enrollment, selectivity in the admissions process, balanced supply of students with various academic and professional interests, a desirable male-to-female ratio, and the like.

Enrollment management may be divided into two broad areas: student recruitment and selection, and retention. In terms of processes, there are the college selection processes, those of students selecting colleges and of colleges selecting students, and the educational process, that of students being educated and retained, from matriculation through graduation. These processes may be successfully studied separately, particularly the college selection processes, or seen as intimately linked; the types of students initially contacted directly affects those who may apply, and thus those who enroll, which in turn affects retention, and finally the types of students who graduate.

Early in the evolution of enrollment management, senior administrators asked themselves, and soon asked their offices of institutional research, questions such as: Can we continue to meet the enrollment target? What will happen to selectivity if the size of the applicant pool diminishes with the "grim demographics?" It soon became apparent that a more sophisticated understanding of the process by which students selected a college was essential if the institution was to manage its enrollment in the face of adverse demographic trends. Questions posed next included ones such as:

1. How can we increase the size of the applicant pool?
2. How can we improve yield?
3. How effective are our existing recruitment activities?
4. Of all the possible tactics for improving student recruitment, which will be the most effective?
5. What aggregate percentage of a freshman class persists to graduation?

Do any student subgroups exhibit significantly higher than average attrition or retention? Why do some students persist while others do not?

More recently, this research agenda has come to include questions about differences among prospective student groups in their responsiveness to various recruitment, enrollment, and retention tactics. Market segmentation has come into its own. The need for more sophisticated research arose from success in answering the first questions and the need to understand the more subtle issues raised by the early answers.

In discussing now the agenda for institutional research as it supports the enrollment management function, it will be useful to divide this entire function into its two broad divisions, student recruitment and retention. Following general lines of historical development, we will first review the research into the college selection process and then briefly discuss student retention.

Academic Market Research: The New Science for Enrollment Management

Over the past decade the emphasis of many institutional research offices has shifted from budget matters to enrollment issues. This shift in emphasis reflects a renewed urgency in meeting enrollment targets and in sustaining or improving the institution's position in an increasingly competitive environment.

In answering the enrollment-oriented questions posed by the enrollment managers, institutional research offices borrowed and adapted methodologies and, to a limited degree, specific findings, from the more advanced market research already developed in the corporate sector. Particularly useful was a rapidly growing subfield known as ''services sector marketing'': the marketing of services, or intangibles, as opposed to the marketing of goods, tangible products, which in most ways are easier to promote. A current treatment of the subject is found in *Services Marketing* (Lovelock, 1984).

However, much of the methodology and nearly all of the results relevant to marketing higher education had to be developed. Higher education research created a myriad of surveys and administered them to the various student populations, their parents, guidance personnel, and so on. Over time the surveys and their administration became more sophisticated. The issues studied grew increasingly subtle as the larger picture became clear. Numerous existing analytical and statistical techniques were borrowed and the survey data subjected to complex analyses. Researchers developed interview techniques for students and their parents, as well as the primary constituencies within higher education institutions. External data resources were tapped, including local and national census data and other demographic profiles. Slowly, higher education became comfortable with terms such as *recruitment, markets, marketing, market share, segmentation, competition, positioning, image analysis*, and so forth. These concepts, once viewed as suspect, have now become commonplace in the halls of academe.

Initially, market research in higher education was highly decentralized and individualistic. However, in only one decade, this always energetic effort has led to the birth, and now the adolescence, of a new applied science, now commonly referred to as "academic market research." Through the work of relatively few professionals such as Kotler and Ihlanfeldt at Northwestern; Litten and Sullivan at Carleton College; McGuire and Lay at Boston College; Lolli at Cornell; Zemsky, Tierney, and others at the University of Pennsylvania; Davis-Van Atta at Oberlin; and certainly a number of others, there now exists a substantial common body of knowledge about the college selection process, knowledge that has been applied with significant success to student recruitment at a variety of institutions.

Stages in the College Selection Process

The college selection process may usefully be divided into three distinct stages: the inquiry stage, the application stage, and the enrollment stage. We will examine each of these stages from the perspectives of three groups: prospective students, those responsible for the institution's enrollment management program, and the institutional research officer. The college selection process looks rather different from each of these perspectives. Each student seeks to find that single institution, from among over three thousand colleges and universities in the United States, that best fits that student's personal and educational objectives. Each institution's enrollment managers seek to enroll that group of students, from among nearly 1.5 million college-bound high school seniors, who can best benefit from that institution's educational program. The institutional research officer seeks to understand and model these processes, and thereby to aid the institution in recruiting its student body.

From a conceptual standpoint, these stages might better be termed *decision processes*: the inquiry decision process, the application decision process, and the enrollment decision process. All three require that choices be made by prospective students and that they be made over time, which must be understood if students are to be influenced favorably by a successful enrollment management effort. Therefore, it is important for both the enrollment management and the research officers to see the research effort as the attempt to understand the people and forces that shape these decisions and how these interact and change with time. Understanding must be developed of the individuals involved in making the choices, what information they use, and how the alternatives are identified, selected, and eliminated.

Each of these three decision subprocesses will now be considered separately. Before beginning, however, it should be noted that we will not attempt to detail specifically the information that academic market research has gathered about these stages. Limitations of space prohibit this, and each institution must tailor its research program to its own individual mission and markets. Rather, we will sketch the key questions about each of the stages that need to be answered by institutional research, and we will suggest some methods to gain those answers.

The Inquiry Decision Process. The secondary school student's initial task is to narrow the number of possible institutions from over three thousand to a significantly smaller number for more detailed investigation. In doing so, the student acquires information about higher education generally and about specific institutions: their programs, costs, reputations, characters, and cultures. The student also assesses the likelihood of admission to specific colleges, or types of colleges, in light of his or her qualifications.

The inquiry decision process is the least well researched of the three. Nevertheless, it is the one at which nearly all institutions are excluded from the choice set of an individual college-bound student. The number of inquiries individual colleges may receive each year ranges from fewer than ten thousand to something more than a hundred thousand. However, since roughly 1.5 million new freshmen enter higher education each year, most never inquire to any given institution. The inquiry stage is the least well researched for good reasons—it is difficult to study. It takes place over a very long period of time (from a student's preteen years to the senior year in high school), it involves a highly dispersed clientele possessing a wide variety of characteristics and attitudes, and it is subject to direct and indirect influence by the many people and forces that surround rapidly maturing young adults.

In spite of its lower research profile, there are certain issues clearly foremost at this stage. The first might be characterized as determining who the students forming what we will call the "realistic market" are. What are the objective, external characteristics and the internal, subjective attitudes, needs, desires, and so on of the population that will be well served by a specific institution and that the school also has a reasonable chance of attracting? From the enrollment management perspective, questions to be addressed in defining the realistic market primarily involve those related to institutional mission:

1. What age range does the institution aim to educate?
2. Which academic and professional fields of interest is it prepared to serve?
3. Over what geographic area can it reasonably expect to attract students?
4. What is the academic aptitude profile of the students it desires to enroll and is prepared to educate?
5. What is the socioeconomic profile of such students and families?
6. How much are they willing to pay for the type and quality of education offered?

Some of the questions used to define the realistic market will be answered internally, such as the academic and professional interests catered to by the institution. Others, such as the financial resources available and which families will choose to pay for a particular type of education, will prove more elusive as research issues. Nevertheless, defining the institution's realistic market is an essential first step.

Most institutions have at least some intuitive sense of the prospective students comprising their realistic market, but few understand their potential markets from the objective standpoint, from the vantage of explicit and quantitative study and definition. Here is an excellent example of the principle that information enables influence: Those institutions that accurately define their potential markets can gain a significant advantage over the competition. Such informed schools will not have to spread their efforts over unrealistic, unproductive markets. They can concentrate their efforts where return on their recruitment investments will be greatest.

Once the realistic market or markets are defined and identified, the second step is to understand them. The basic question for institutional research in support of the enrollment management effort at the inquiry stage is: Why do some students in the realistic market inquire while others do not? The first step in answering this question concerns institutional visibility. Who knows of the school? What percentage recognizes the institution's name? How many know at least something about the school beyond its name? One thing is certain: If a student or family has not heard of an institution, they can never inquire. Assessing institutional visibility is the necessary first step.

After visibility comes institutional image. How does the realistic market (the students who recognize the institution) see it? What characteristics are viewed positively? What are the most attractive features? The strengths? What are the weaker, less attractive attributes? The specific dimensions chosen on which to study institutional image must, to some degree, be determined by the special characteristics of a given institution and, to some degree, must explore issues well established to be common in the college selection process of essentially all college-bound students and their families.

Once an assessment of image is completed, a key issue becomes the degree to which image matches reality. On which characteristics is the institution perceived accurately? On which is there clearly misconception in the minds of the realistic prospective market? A marketing program may then be guided knowledgeably by this information to address the specific image issues. The data collected concerning institutional image must be widely disseminated and understood throughout the institution. While it is critical to those involved in recruitment strategy, publications, and public relations, image assessment is most effective when the results are broadly known by all campus constituencies, since enrollment management is by its nature necessarily a function of the entire institution.

Another question relevant to image studies concerns assessing market potential for the institution. The previous question examined the match between image and fact. Market potential concerns the match between institutional reality and market reality: the nature of the school and what it offers in relation to what benefits and services potential clientele desire. This issue is relevant not only to those segments of the market that recognize a school but also to those that do not. Determining specific consumer demands for education within the realistic market is a necessary step before assuming an institution can expand its appeal successfully into untapped markets. Once the specific benefits and services are known, those in fact offered may be promoted most actively in order to maximize the response to the recruitment efforts. The marketing program will be guided by sound information.

These are not simple issues, and their study is both theoretically and practically complex. Nevertheless, there are ways to begin such analyses. One good method for those institutions using direct mail is to survey a sample of students who were mailed promotional materials but never responded to these appeals. These non-inquirants form an excellent test group for assessing institutional image, benefits, and services desired in education and, to a lesser degree, institutional visibility. Since names and addresses are readily available, it is a relatively simple matter to survey this population to study these issues. In doing so, always bear in mind that the overarching question for the research effort at this stage should be: Why do certain students in the realistic market inquire while others do not?

Another method for studying the inquiry decision is the personal interview. This is particularly well adapted to institutions serving a relatively small, well-defined geographic area. A number of two-year community colleges have become adept at this method. Various local public and private agencies may be able to provide mailing lists of local residents, perhaps refined to include only those fitting certain criteria, if so desired.

Study of the inquiry decision is more difficult, however, for institutions with statewide, regional, or national appeal, or for those seeking to expand into new geographic markets. Here the field of academic market research is not as advanced as elsewhere. Decent first-order data exist on the services and benefits sought in a college education among various subgroups of the college-bound population (see Litten and others, 1983). But good data specific to individual institutions are scant. Typically, these must be gathered through private market research firms, a growing number of which have departments specializing in research for colleges and universities.

The Application Decision Process. Following the inquiry decision comes the second major stage in college selection: the application decision process. For the student, who by this point has gathered information about a variety of colleges and clarified attitudes and beliefs about a college education, the decision now is choosing the school or schools at which to apply. For the enrollment management program, the primary issue is how most effectively to deploy resources so as to convert desirable inquirants into applicants. For the research program, the fundamental question is: Why do certain inquirants apply while others do not.

Research is more easily conducted at this stage. Names and addresses of all inquirants are readily available (providing the admissions office maintains scrupulous records of all inquirants, now a fundamental prerequisite for effective enrollment management). Additional data are equally important at this stage. Characteristics such as academic interest, geographic location, sex, ethnic background, SAT and ACT scores, proxies for socioeconomic status, and the specific methods and publications used in recruitment are likely to be available wholly or in part. These provide several dimensions on which to divide the total inquiry population into its different segments, a necessary part of market research today.

When contrasted with the inquiry decision process, the application decision process typically occurs in a more orderly manner. The alternatives are fewer, and the amount of information about each alternative is greater. The application decision process is therefore generally more explicit and conscious; it occurs within a relatively well-defined and limited time frame. For these reasons, research is more readily conducted on this phase of the college selection. Consequently, more institutions have conducted studies on this stage, and more is known about it. The primary research method remains the written survey mailed to various inquiry populations. However, telephone surveys and personal interviews, typically conducted by independent third parties, have also been increasingly employed in recent years.

In addressing the fundamental research issue concerning the application decision—why certain inquirants apply and others do not—the written questionnaire (mailed to both applicants and nonapplicants) is the primary method employed. The following questions would be among the first to be answered by the office of institutional research:

1. Among all inquirants, do there exist differences in rates of conversion into applicants that may be attributed to important characteristics such as sex, geography, academic interest, methods or publications used in recruitment, or ethnic background? If so, can it be determined from on-campus data why such differences exist? If not (as will be the usual case), the reasons underlying the differential conversion rates become key issues for subsequent research.

2. Among the nonapplicants, what general characteristics about colleges are rated most and least attractive? What portion of the nonapplicant group is a realistic market to attempt to attract as applicants? What benefits and services are applicants seeking in an education? How do the attributes they rate as highly attractive and the most important benefits and services sought fit in with the nature of the institution?

3. What is the academic potential in the nonapplicant group (typically measured by standardized test scores and high school performance)? What is their general descriptive profile? What are their aspirations and needs in a college education? And what percentage of them is likely to be successful academically?

4. How well aware of the institution are these well-disposed, realistic nonapplicants? Given their contact with the school and vice versa, do they clearly recall the institution's name? How well do they believe they have come to know the school? How accurate, in fact, is their knowledge? If their knowledge is vague or inaccurate, perhaps more detailed written materials or additional facts presented during face-to-face contacts would convince them to apply. If they have come to know the institution well and accurately but have decided

not to apply, expanding significantly into their markets may well prove difficult and costly.

5. Almost explicit by this last point is, once again, the requirement of making an accurate assessment of institutional image as held by the well-disposed, realistic nonapplicant. Where is it accurate and inaccurate? If the inaccuracies could be corrected by more effective communications, would this be likely to convert more of these inquirants into applicants? That is, would the institutional offerings and general nature, if better communicated, fit in more closely with the benefits, services, and general characteristics desired in a college by those who inquired but did not apply?

6. What is the timing of the application decision? At which point in time following initial inquiry did the nonapplicant exclude the institution from his or her narrowing set of choices? This is a critical assessment to make. The college selection process is, foremost, a process. It occurs over time, and choices must be made throughout. Once made, these choices tend to be irreversible. Attempting to convince inquirants to apply may work best for certain college-bound students and certain institutions during a December through February period but will not work at all after October for others. One must be certain not to wait in employing the primary recruitment tactics beyond the point that a majority of the prospective market has made its decisions concerning where to apply.

Equally important, one must not attempt to strike before the iron is hot. Recruiting too early, before markets are receptive, will be unproductive and costly. The research program should seek to determine when the various segments of the nonapplying inquiry pool indicate that they excluded the institution from their choice set. Note that the decision process itself actually occurs shortly before this time, since what respondents report on a questionnaire conducted well after the fact is the point at which the decision was finally made.

7. How did the nonapplicant group go about the process of identifying and choosing from among the options for a college education? What information sources were used? Were different sources employed to learn about certain aspects, for example the academic ones as opposed to others? How valuable were these various sources; that is, what credence is placed on various information sources? Who is trusted? Were different sources used in assessing this institution as opposed to those employed in learning about the competition? What was the image portrayed to inquirants through various sources? How attractive did the school appear as viewed through the many lenses used by prospectives?

8. Last, but definitely not least, who is the competition for the well-disposed, realistic nonapplicants? Specifically, to which colleges and universities did they apply? To which were they admitted? Where did they enroll? Most admissions officers have an intuitive sense for the names and nature of the competing institutions and, thereby, for the characteristics of the students choosing them. However, it is essential that the marketing effort have explicit knowledge of who the competition is.

For the enrollment management program, the other critical question in the competition analyses is: Is it realistic to attempt to recruit a substantial portion of the nonapplicants away from the competing schools to which they have already decided to apply? The importance of examining the competitive structure for the nonapplicants and of making a realistic assessment of the institution's ability to compete before attempting to convert significant numbers of nonapplicants into the applicant pool cannot be overstated.

This is a long shopping list. It is one intended for the whole of academic market research, not for any one institution. A specific market research project will be required to pick and choose from these questions those most relevant to the institution. Embedded within this outline of the general first issues lie all the specific ones, such as the role of various adult influences at this stage (parents, guidance personnel, friends of the family, high school teachers, employers), the role of alumni, the influences of gross costs and the availability of financial aid, the role of geography and distance from home, and the influence of peers.

The Enrollment Decision Process. The third and final stage of college selection is the enrollment decision process. For the student this translates as selecting the one school in which to enroll from among all those that have offered admission. For the enrollment management effort, the issue is how best to influence the enrollment decision. The fundamental institutional research objective is to understand why some admitted students choose to enroll while the remainder do not.

The enrollment decision was the stage explored first by most institutional market research efforts. It is the stage most easily investigated. The population is relatively small and clearly defined. Admitted students' greater familiarity with specific schools and direct experience with college admissions processes make research into the subtle, but often important, issues easier. Their greater involvement with the institution makes admitted students a more responsive population. Through the application process, the institution is likely to have available a great deal of objective (perhaps even some attitudinal) data about those offered admission. The enrollment decision process is therefore the most researched and, in many ways, the best understood.

Here again the direct mail survey is the primary research technique, though other methods have been applied at this stage. Many of the research issues central to the application decision are also relevant here:

- Desired benefits and services sought in a college education; the most important attributes about colleges at this stage
- Timing of the decision
- Institutional images held of the attributes considered most important and how those images were formed; what information sources were used
- The fit between images and the reality of the institution
- The fit between the institutional character and offerings and those sought by the prospective student

- And last, but quite likely first in importance, the structure of the competition.

Despite the similarities in the questions to be examined, academic market research has found consistent differences between the first two stages of college selection and the last one. Certainly, the range of students involved is narrow. The timing is obviously later. More importantly, the salient factors and forces influencing the enrollment decision process are often different as well. Costs and parents (and adults in general) are usually found to be less important to the enrollment decision than they were earlier. In some studies, geographical location and distance from home appear to play reduced roles. In general, this final decision is often found to rest less on the institutional attributes rated most important and more on the less central, highly individual factors.

The apparently contradictory results make sense on the following analysis. At the point of making the enrollment decision, the student has honed the roughly three thousand United States colleges and universities down to a very limited set. Those not rated highly on the most important factors have been eliminated in the first two stages. The final choice set (of genuine interest) is likely to contain fairly similar institutions. Thus, the enrollment decision process tends to be dominated by relatively slight perceived differences between a few institutions, differences that at earlier stages may not have been rated as highly important, but that now enter the decision process as determinative.

This leads directly to the final point concerning the agenda for the institutional research effort in support of an enrollment management program. In studying the enrollment decision, the overriding concern is the competition. Nearly all students who do not enroll at a given institution have decided to enroll somewhere else. If a school is to influence favorably the enrollment decisions of those whom it admits, it must, in effect, persuade them to abandon the competitors most often chosen by other highly similar students.

The research implications of the requirement for thorough competition analysis at this stage are numerous. However, two stand out:

1. All institutional image analyses must be made relative to the image of the competition. In examining how the school is perceived on any given characteristic, one must also assess how the competition is rated.

2. Quite likely the most important research issue at this stage is the objective structure of the competition: To which other institutions do admitted students most often apply? To which are they admitted? And what percentage of students selects us over the competitors? Such study in the secular marketing world would be referred to as the objective study of consumer behavior. At this stage, what students do can be as important and illuminating, if not more so, than the reasons why they do so. (See Zemsky and Oedel, 1983, for a treatment of the geographic and socioeconomic determinants of early college selection behavior and the resultant interinstitutional patterns of competition viewed from the national perspective.)

Studying the patterns of competition (for a selective, private college), over the decade of the 1980s has yielded a wealth of interesting and useful data.

But the most important picture that emerges is one of remarkable stability. Every year, Oberlin College competes for admitted students with virtually the same set of institutions. Even more important, the volume of overlap with each changes only slightly from year to year. The primary competitors this year are identically those of five years ago with at most modest changes in rank ordering. Subsequently, each year most competitors admit roughly the same percentages of cross-applicants as in previous years. And, in the end, what may be termed the *draw ratios* (the percentages of mutually admitted students that select Oberlin over the competition) also change little from one year to the next.

All this is despite the fact that many schools are increasing their recruiting efforts for these students. Many are using market research data on the enrollment decision in attempting to influence greater proportions to enroll. However, not all schools in the competition set are doing so. Yet, for all our individual and collective efforts, not much changes! The overall yield of admitted students appears to be predominantly a function of highly stable application overlap patterns. Perceived differences in institutional quality and attractiveness doubtlessly contribute substantially both to application overlap and to draw ratios, but these appear to change little and only very slowly. (This is not to suggest that change is impossible.)

Therefore, if an institution wishes to make a substantive improvement in its enrolled student body, improvement on a scale sufficient to cope with demographic changes or to improve its competitive position, the most effective method may be to recruit an applicant population that is more likely to overlap with a set of competing schools against which the institution usually "wins." That is, they will successfully turn these applicants into matriculants. If yield is a function of application overlap, then the management of yield must primarily involve the management of that overlap. This more strategic view represents a significant departure from the traditional, purely tactical approaches that have rested almost exclusively on attempting to alter the highly stable draw ratios. We believe it offers considerably greater promise.

Retention: The Persistence Decision Process

Enrollment management, and consequently its research component, has come relatively late to the subject of retention as one for serious consideration. Within the framework adopted here, we view retention and its converse, attrition, as outcomes of an ongoing persistence decision process. The research issues and findings are less advanced concerning this important area of enrollment management.

First, it is instructive to place persistence in a numerical context from the enrollment manager's perspective. Every additional student retained until graduation is one fewer student the admissions effort must enroll. Depending on the yield percentage for admitted applicants, one fewer newly enrolled student translates into perhaps two to four fewer who must be admitted. This, in turn, means perhaps four, five, or more applicants who need not be recruited (though this is not to recommend lessening recruitment efforts). Finally, these translate into as many as forty inquirants who need not be generated. Numerically, significant improvement in retention makes an obvious impact on the recruitment effort.

Despite its importance, many institutions have only lately viewed retention as a key component of enrollment management. Clearly, it is a difficult area of research. Withdrawal decicisions especially are highly subject to rationalization, potentially biasing responses to queries about the reasons for departure. While rationalization is certainly a troublesome issue for college selection research, it is particularly so for retention research.

From the institutional research perspective, the first step is to determine who is and who is not graduating, according to as many objective characteristics as possible. The obvious ones are those of sex, age, ethnic background, academic major, academic aptitude and performance, distance from home, parental education levels, family income, and financial aid status. Such studies may suggest some possible reasons for persistence or identify certain target populations for potential intervention. However, most such studies have not illuminated the primary underlying causes of either persistence or withdrawal. The subject of student retention is very complex. (See Chapter Four in this issue for a more detailed discussion of the subject.)

There is one effective method for reducing the otherwise enormous task of investigating retention and attrition. It is best described as a method of conceiving of the persistence decision process. This decision process can usefully be considered akin to a cost-benefit analysis. There are numerous benefits to a college education and experience. (Recall that benefits sought form a primary basis for the decisions made during the college selection process.) There are also equally as many associated costs of an education. Financial cost is only one among many. Students will persist so long as the perceived benefits being received outweigh the perceived costs involved in receiving them. When the balance shifts in favor of perceived costs, the student will leave.

This analysis is not to suggest that the persistence decision process is as logical and clear-cut as other cost-benefit ratios. It is very often subjective, implicit, illogical, or even subliminal. These traits make it a challenging subject for research. Under this conception of the process, however, the research issues become ones such as discovering the perceived benefits and costs of attending an institution, the various weights different types of students give to these, how these weights change from the beginning of freshman year through the beginning of junior year (the period of greatest attrition), and how these costs, benefits, and weights are the same and different among persisting students and permanent dropouts.

Finally, there is for the retention research agenda the analogue of the objective analysis of consumer behavior so essential to an understanding of the enrollment decision. With retention, this question is: Among students who leave, what do they do after departure? Do they continue higher education and, if so, do they do so eventually or immediately? Do they leave to enter the work force rather than continue their education? For those who continue education, what schools do they select? Are these schools larger or smaller? Less expensive or more so? Closer to home or farther away? Less or more academically rigorous? Do they offer certain academic majors not available locally? Does a potential mate attend the institution? If patterns can be found in the objective choices made by various types of departing students, these may illuminate the underlying reasons for departure at least as well as, and perhaps better than, all the subjective data and theoretical analyses one might otherwise employ.

Enrollment Management and Institutional Research: An Effective Partnership

The final topic concerns the nature of the partnership between the enrollment management program and the institutional research officer. If that partnership is to be effective, both sides must recognize clearly their proper roles. We have stressed that information enables influence. The information and analyses the institutional research officer brings to the enrollment management effort potentially enable him or her to influence the policies adopted by the enrollment management program. In that prospect lies the potential to enhance enrollment management success as well as possible difficulty, for as useful and factual as data can be, they are equally and unavoidably political.

Sound data collection and solid policy analysis are essential to effective enrollment management. However, numbers can be shaped to build a very convincing case. Computer printouts can gain a life and truth of their own. Enrollment management policy makers must be certain not to ask or allow research personnel to become decision makers. Research must not be guided by preconceived policy preferences or axes to be ground. A prerequisite for the effective use of institutional research is the solid conviction that the research reports are grounded in objective facts, untainted by bias. Given this conviction, the institution can employ institutional research to enable informed choices to be made that improve its enrollment management. However, it is imperative that final responsibility for all decisions be retained by the enrollment manager and others directly charged with the success of the management effort. The research officer, while providing as much useful information, analyses, and conclusions as possible, should remain detached from the final authority for decisions in order to ensure objectivity in work and in the campus perception thereof.

References

Litten, L. H., Sullivan, D., and Brodigan, D. L. *Applying Market Research in College Admissions.* New York: College Entrance Examination Board, 1983.

Lovelock, C. H. *Services Marketing.* Englewood Cliffs, N.J.: Prentice-Hall, 1984.

Zemsky, R., and Oedel, P. *The Structure of College Choice.* New York: College Entrance Examination Board, 1983.

David L. Davis-Van Atta is director of institutional research at Oberlin College, in Oberlin, Ohio.

Sam C. Carrier is provost at Oberlin College and is in charge of the planning function.

The various parties that can contribute to the enrollment
management effort at a college must be brought together.

Organizing the Resources
That Can Be Effective

A. Steven Graff

One of the great challenges—or nightmares—of our present period of academic history is enrollment management (Trachtenberg, 1984). Most institutions of higher education have realized the need to emerge from the ivory tower and recognize the importance of considering the world around them. Many presidents and provosts, however, have been slow to see the profound implications of the new demographic and financial realities and, therefore, have been slow to alter the foci of their attention and management efforts (Keller, 1985). It has been said (Graff, 1985, p. 5), that "most institutions remain a collection of fiefdoms with little focus or coordination: each office must serve while at the same time demanding service from others. Faculty function like knights: offering service but not necessarily commitment or allegiance. Moving such a feudal organism . . . is an Arthurian task."

This is not an encouraging picture, but the model that has been outlined in the previous chapters offers hope that institutions of higher education can be in a position to take some command of their destinies. The enrollment management model is a very rational one, grounded in fairly expansively documented theory. And, although at least some authors (Cohen and March, 1974) have suggested that colleges and universities do not use rational decision-making models, it appears that more than a handful of institutions are at least exploring how they might translate the term. One need only look through a section

D. Hossler (Ed.), *Managing College Enrollments.* New Directions for
Higher Education, no. 53. San Francisco: Jossey-Bass, March 1986.

of administrative position listings to realize that enrollment management positions are appearing with more and more frequency. While it is still fairly clear that enrollment management as it has been presented here is not fully comprehended (Novak and Weiss, 1985), more and more institutions are asking "how to" questions.

Unfortunately, there is not just one way to incorporate the enrollment management model into an existing organizational structure. A number of institutions have tried to simply change position titles. Others have taken two or three obviously complementary administrative functions and combined them under one umbrella. What has not been realized, however, is that institutions must consciously organize themselves to manage their enrollments. Such organization offers both opportunity and challenge, which come as the institution formulates an enrollment management structure fitting its own style and personality. The various campus activities that are included will depend on how the institution sees itself and its future.

The activities to be included as part of enrollment management are not universally agreed on but generally tend to include: marketing, recruitment, admissions, orientation, financial aid, academic support and development programs, academic advising, registration, retention, career planning and placement, and student services (Kemerer and others, 1982; Chatham, 1985; Hossler, 1984; Kennedy, 1984). Other functions that have been mentioned for inclusion are: institutional research, academic program evaluation and development, long-range planning, price setting, and clarification of institutional mission. In more generic terms, enrollment management includes all activities focused on recruiting, admitting, funding, tracking, retaining, and replacing students (Rainsford, 1985). Chapter One of this volume discusses a list of potential activities that may suggest some organizational imperatives for enrollment management on an individual campus.

Bringing together a combination of functional activities seems appropriate from an institutional perspective of enrollment management, but it is no simple task. There is no template that can be laid over an existing organizational structure to outline how the enrollment management function should be drawn. There are examples in the literature of individual institutional restructurings (Kreutner and Godfrey, 1980–81; Kennedy, 1984; Huddleston, 1984; Rainsford, 1985), but one must be cautioned that there is no evidence of the appropriateness of these in other settings. Even the archetypal models of enrollment management organization outlined by Kemerer and others (1982)—the committee, the coordinator, and the matrix or division—and discussed fully in Chapter One do not provide for all of the possible idiosyncratic differences that exist from one campus to another. Perhaps a way of approaching the structural organization of an enrollment management team will be illuminated by considering the various functional units that might be included.

Potential Players for the Enrollment Management Team

The administrative officers and managers, not to mention the faculty of a collegiate institution, represent a collection of personalities with differing skills, backgrounds, allegiances, obligations, and ambitions. Their tasks are generally functionally well defined and often prescribed not only by educational tradition and protocol but by the political infrastructure of the particular campus. Although it would be preferable to be able to factor these local campus opportunities and limitations into our discussion, what follows is a review of potential players for an enrollment management team general enough to permit translation to most institutional settings. Realizing this need to read from one's own institutional perspective, I hope the following comments will help to focus consideration of various campus resources.

The Chief Executive Officer. Most authors on the topic of enrollment management have acknowledged the importance of the involvement of the chief executive officer, or president, to any successful program. The nature of that involvement, however, is often viewed quite differently. Does the president function in fact as the enrollment manager, coordinating the efforts of a variety of the institution's academic and administrative personnel? Does the president make certain the combination of human and organizational resources is present to ensure an effective enrollment management effort? Does the president maintain an awareness of the institution's enrollment management efforts but not get directly involved? Does the president delegate all enrollment management responsibility to others and simply provide support and assistance when requested? Any of these descriptions provide a definition of positive involvement.

The president cannot abdicate all involvement if efforts to manage enrollments are to succeed. Support from the top is critical if for no other reason than the fact that the presidential imprimatur encourages favorable support from all parts of the institution. Probably one of the most useful things a president can do is encourage the involvement of others in the enrollment management effort. Although there can be a negative side to encouraging involvement—second guessing—the president's support can help to minimize it. Whether it is in a directive role or simply one of providing active support, the leadership provided by the president will establish the tone and provide a strong measure of credibility for the enrollment management effort.

Chief Academic Officer. The provost or vice-president for academic affairs can and probably should be one of the key figures involved in enrollment management efforts. As the administrator most directly connected with the faculty, the chief academic officer is in a position to affect a variety of areas important in influencing enrollments. Within the purview of the chief academic officer are the development, encouragement, and evaluation of the academic program; the structuring and monitoring of academic advising; and the organization, staffing, and evaluation of academic support and development programs.

In many cases, he or she will also be actively involved in the personnel decisions affecting faculty and many of the administrators generally viewed as part of the enrollment management team.

Because of the day-to-day involvement that the chief academic officer has with so many of the programs and personnel dealing with enrollment-related areas, his or her influence and support can be a major factor in the realization and maintenance of an effective enrollment management effort. Helping the faculty to understand the relationship between the academic program and enrollment levels or, more directly, helping to convince the faculty that enrollments and such things as salary, teaching load, tenure, and number of positions are directly related can positively affect the atmosphere in which the enrollment management team must function. Encouraging and even rewarding faculty members for their involvement in activities directly related to enrollment management can alleviate much of the institutional inertia that often plagues new endeavors.

On the administrative side, the chief academic officer may frequently be the best-positioned institutional official to bring together most of the players involved in the enrollment management team. His or her influence and positive support can go a long way in facilitating the interaction of the various units and managers, regardless of the organizational structure being implemented. The chief academic officer will also have to provide much of the direction for bringing the goals and activities of the various units into congruence with the enrollment objectives of the campus as a whole.

Chief Admissions Officer. Because of his or her responsibility for marketing, recruitment, and admissions, the chief admissions officer is sometimes viewed as the campus enrollment manager. On some campuses the establishment of an enrollment management system consists of employing a new chief admissions officer with a successful "track record" and generously increasing the admissions budget (Hossler, 1984). On many campuses in which enrollment management means making up in new students for the enrollment lost through graduation and attrition, the chief admissions officer is coming to have something in common with coaches—job security and overall performance rating may be the function of a successful season (Kemerer and others, 1982). Although some admissions practitioners have the broader vision and influence necessary for overall leadership, and many admissions offices do a superb job of meeting whatever new student goals are set, chief admissions officers are most important to enrollment management activities because of the specialized expertise they bring to the overall function.

Traditionally, admissions officers have been viewed as the institutional sales force—employing a variety of techniques to entice whatever students they can find to the campus. Today, the admissions officer must employ a variety of sophisticated and well-planned activities designed to focus on prospective students who by virtue of their preparation, interests, aspirations, and socioeconomic characteristics are most likely to be predisposed toward their institution. Writings such as Manski and Wise (1983) and Zemsky and Oedel (1983) and services such as the College Board's Enrollment Planning Service and ACT's Enrollment Information Service provide a wealth of information and a better understanding of the college choice process. The expertise in and understanding of marketing, direct-mail solicitation, telemarketing, advertising, and consultative selling is what makes the chief admissions officer a potentially valuable member of the enrollment management team.

Numbers are not the only concern of the chief admissions officer. More and more institutions are now asking for specific kinds of students to fill their classrooms. This is quite a challenge if the institution has not organized itself to concentrate on broader enrollment concerns and looks only to admissions to maintain gross enrollment stability. The ability to select an incoming class appropriate in size and composition to the desires of the institution is becoming the true challenge in admissions and reflects quite clearly the basic emphasis of enrollment management as presented in this volume. In many ways the chief admissions officer stands to benefit the most from an organized enrollment management effort; tasks will be better and more realistically defined, and there will be support from the other key players on the team.

Financial Aid Officer. Of all the potential players on an enrollment management team, the financial aid officer is possibly the most illusive in terms of how his or her function can be described. To many, the financial aid officer is a part of the business side of the administration, laboring over fiscal reports and maintaining an array of programs that are voluminously regulated and subject to routine audit. Others view the financial aid operation as a student service, providing students with assistance and aid to enable them to matriculate and progress through the institutional offerings. A third view, and the one probably most closely related to enrollment management, sees financial aid as a tool for encouraging students to enroll and assisting them to persist to graduation. This is perhaps the least accepted but potentially the most strategic role a financial aid officer can play. Without this perspective an enrollment management effort cannot succeed. In reality a good financial aid officer must include each of these roles in this operation, with the particular blend being the critical element in determining how successfully the operation meets institutional needs.

One of the real frustrations many financial aid officers face is the fact that they are usually seen in a serving rather than a leading role. Regardless of which niche they have been placed in organizationally, they generally must work to meet the goals of others rather than to participate in the establishment of broader institutional goals. Johnstone and Huff (1983) suggest five functions of the financial aid administrator: serving students, informing the institutional community about aid issues, promoting the program's efficiency, ensuring the program's integrity, and educating students and others about financial aid philosophies and practices. Tierney (1985) has suggested a new role for this list, that of serving as a clearinghouse for student financial planning in order to ensure access to capital to assist in financing higher education. Is it any wonder financial aid officers are often less than enthusiastic and are unsure about new ways of reorganizing the structure in which they function?

Student Affairs Officer. Student affairs officers manage a broad variety of functional units often referred to as student services. These units are usually described on organizational charts by a horizontal or "flat" pattern, with all major services reporting to the chief student affairs organizer. As Dutton and Rickard (1980, p. 389) put it, "The organization of the student services program is . . . a system of learning support services designed to help students clarify and attain their educational objectives." Although in recent times (Miller and Prince, 1976) student services have been described in philosophical terms that seem to place them beyond the day-to-day mission of the institution, an insightful author (Ambler, 1980) is quick to point out the need for their compatibility with institutional goals. This is often perceived by student affairs officers as a functional dichotomy between the role of educator and practitioner, with the former being considered more professional, since it is supported by a systematic body of knowledge based on theoretical constructs. While the significance of the educator role is compelling, the student affairs division must contribute to the enrollment management effort of the institution.

The chief student affairs officer should be considered as the broker of a wide variety of contributing activities important to enrollment management. Generally described as a group of facilitating and developmental programs and activities, these contributing activities have been grouped functionally into nine areas: academic support, recreation and culture, financial aid, housing and food service, mental health, physical health, special services, student activities and government, and research and needs assessment (Dutton and Rickard, 1980). Such activities can play an important role in shaping the attractiveness of the institution to high school students, as well as enhancing student persistence after matriculation. The student affairs officer can use his or her knowledge as an educator to focus these services as a practitioner on the meeting of specific institutional objectives.

Institutional Researcher. Whether an administrator with a specific institutional research title, a faculty member with an interest in doing functional research, or an external consultant, the institutional researcher is a critical player if enrollment management is being taken seriously. Davis-Van Atta (1985) states that the basic function of the institutional researcher is "to provide you (enrollment manager) with the information and understanding necessary to influence the processes controlling the quantity and quality of your enrollments." Some of the information topics important to the institutional researcher (Braxton, 1984) are: student characteristics and the college choice process, assessments of the competition, and the efficacy of recruitment activities. The basic reasons for researching these topics is to provide a medium for testing "truth claims" regarding institutional processes and activities. This research is necessary because people have a tendency to presuppose validity prior to empirical validation and generally to let it direct their actions, rather than taking the time to find out the actual facts.

The institutional researcher is probably the potential team member least often found on our campuses. For a variety of reasons, research has often been left up to individual unit managers with the result that there is seldom any systematic logic to the information being collected and analyzed. The trend in recent years has been to utilize the services of outside research and marketing firms to do much of the research in support of the marketing and recruitment-admissions function, while studies of campus populations have been left to individual administrative practitioners. With few exceptions faculty members have been infrequently disposed to turning their attentions to subjects close at hand. This generally has been the result of an attitude on the part of the faculty that enrollment management and the information that supports it is someone else's concern. Kemerer and others (1982) argue that this myopic view has been reinforced by the growing use of external researchers. If a campus is seriously considering moving toward enrollment management, the area of institutional research and how it is organized should be one of the first areas addressed.

Registrar. Once an integral part of the gatekeeping triumvirate—admissions, financial aid, and registration—the registrar has become the least considered and often one of the least understood administrative officers on campus. Growing functional specialization has contributed to the separation of these three functions, which in their frequently common pasts have epitomized the essence of enrollment management. It has been suggested (Kemerer and others, 1982, p. 46) that this "specialization has tended to exacerbate the breakdown in communication among officers concerned with enrollment management."

The registrar can and should be viewed as much more than the mere controller of the credit hour. In fact, the registrar is a conductor, overseeing the blending of students with programs to achieve harmonious results. Rainsford (1985) suggests that the enrollment process can be viewed as an hourglass, with admissions and registrar as the responsible contributors on opposite sides of matriculation. In this illustration the registrar is responsible for the movement of students from the freshman year to graduation, the ins and outs of the transfer process, the movement of students among majors, and retention. In many cases the registrar is also the guardian of the institution's facts and lore that support and direct the researcher's task. If one gives these ideas some thought, it is not difficult to see the potential contributions a registrar could make to an enrollment management team.

Other Players. Depending on institutional personalities and structure, a variety of other players might be considered for inclusion on the enrollment management team. The *business officer* is often intimately involved in decisions regarding pricing and financial aid and is also the overseer of a myriad of auxiliary services that affect students daily—buildings and grounds, campus employment, the bookstore, and so on. The *public relations officer* bears ultimate responsibility for the translation of the institutional image to both internal and external publics. This role, which can be one of either coordination or total direction, can strongly influence the perceptions that color the sphere in which enrollment management must operate. The *alumni officer* can also effect the enrollment management sphere, moving among the institution's most vocal and influential public. The education and nurturing of a satisfied and accurately informed alumni can be a major factor in the success of an enrollment management effort. The lack of or failure of such efforts will usually prove to be a major obstacle. *Students* themselves can also play an important role in enrollment management. As reflectors and evaluators of the institution's efforts, students are often able to provide relevant and meaningful insights into the real factors that exert the greatest influence on an institution's success or lack thereof.

By now it should be clear that enrollment management is not something that can be accomplished by one individual or unit on the campus. If it is effective (Rainsford, 1985), the enrollment management effort will be a form of synergism—the actions of more than one organism achieve an effect that would be impossible for any one organism to achieve alone. The individual charged with leading the institution's enrollment management efforts will need to have a broad understanding of the strengths and contributions of each of these potential players. Such an understanding necessitates a breadth of experience and training that is often viewed as nontraditional or unscholarly. In many cases the enrollment management leader will of necessity be a new breed of administrator, possessing an awareness of the institution as a single organizational organism that needs cultivation and nurturing to achieve its fullest potential. Having looked at the activities and players that could be involved, we can now consider how their organization might be approached.

Some Organizational Considerations

Just as there is no one best form of organization, there is no one unique mix of players that can guarantee the successful realization of a managed enrollment. Without a doubt, there are certain functional units and players whose absence would be obvious. The most appropriate team for an institution, however, is the one that brings together the skills, knowledge, influence, understanding, and vision necessary to lead it. The selection and management of that team is both a challenge and an opportunity. The person responsible for putting it together will be challenged to make decisions that do not just follow the path of least resistance but that recognize the necessity of including the brightest and the best in ideas and personnel regardless of their source or rank. He or she will also have the opportunity to create a new management structure without the theoretical and traditional architecture that often prescribes the form and function of both academic and administrative units. Rainsford (1985, p. 343) expressed it very well when he said, "Colleges must learn to be flexible, idea- as well as action-oriented, willing to take risks and to move, and if one strategy does not work, to drop it and go on to the next based on as much knowledge as can be acquired about the reasons for success or failure." This challenge and opportunity are extremely rare in higher education. And when they are found, they are often abused or sadly ignored.

Perhaps there are some things to be considered from the world of business regarding organizational development and success as we consider how to create an enrollment management team; after all, marketing has proved to be more appropriate and much less onerous than many in academia predicted! Basically, organizations are a living whole whose parts are interlocked in complex patterns, and "the purpose of organizational development is to find the best ways of using human and material resources to solve institutional problems and strengthen operations" (Miller and Prince, 1976, p. 149). Who can argue with that? It describes our institutions and, I hope, outlines what we are all trying to find in enrollment management. We need to be reminded, however, that if we are planning to alter or develop one area within the institution, all actual and possible ties to other areas have to be considered. The thoroughness with which that consideration is done will often mean the difference between a successful and an unsuccessful alteration. The creation of an enrollment management team has to be viewed developmentally.

Peters and Waterman (1982, p. 9) found in their research on America's best-run companies, "that any intelligent approach to organizing had to encompass, and treat as interdependent, at least seven variables: structure, strategy, people, management style, systems and procedures, guiding concepts and shared values, and the present and hoped-for corporate strengths or skills." Condensed into the alliterative McKinsey 7-*S* Framework—strategy, structure, style, systems, staff, skills, shared values—their grounded scheme for providing structure to the task of organizing offers a useful outline for a brief delineation of questions to consider in organizing an enrollment management team. Although Peters and Waterman do not suggest any critical order for the 7-*S*'s, the discussion that follows looks at them hierarchically and directs questions personally to enrollment management professionals.

Strategy. Often confused with tactics, a strategy is a plan focused on an objective, whereas tactics are the means employed to achieve the objective. Does your institution know why it wants to pursue enrollment management? What is the objective being focused on? If your institution is seeking to ensure a stabilized enrollment, you must have a different strategy than if you are wanting to change the make-up of your student body. If you are seeking to do both, that is a different strategy, again. Your strategy will provide a foundation for your consideration of the organization and structure of your enrollment management team.

Shared Values. Each institution can be described by a set of values that exert a degree of influence, greater on some campuses than on others, on the people and systems it employs. These values may or may not be institutionalized in mission or policy statements. In many cases these values are shared by the campus community and result in a high degree of commitment to the institutional task; in others they provide definition that may or may not affect the general operation. Are there particular values on your campus that draw people together? Are there guiding concepts that place limits on your consideration of how you might implement enrollment management? An institution with a

98

sense of mission can dictate rather clearly the characteristics of its potential students and may structure its enrollment management team very differently from one with a less focused set of values. But be careful not to confuse a lesser degree of shared values with a lack of clarity or definition of purpose. One must simply have a sense of how to factor in the extent to which the institution's values will affect a new organizational element.

Systems. Almost every organization, regardless of how large, has a set of standard operating procedures that governs routine and frequent tasks and decisions. Institutions of higher education are no exception. Every one of us can think of a procedure on our campus that seems inconsistent or inflexible and that, when questioned, is defended by saying, "We have always done it that way." Are there procedures and systems on your campus that would directly affect your enrollment management efforts? Can you assess their impact on your initial efforts? Will they present obstacles to your establishment of an enrollment management team and to its future operation? How much opportunity will your new enrollment management team have to modify or institute systems and procedures? Probably the best example of the opportunities and limitations a system can impose on an operation can be visualized by considering your own relationship with the data-processing and information systems function on your campus. The operational environment that exists on your campus may be either a positive or a negative factor to be considered as you put together your team. Your assessment of its influences may assist in determining who you need to have on the team.

Style. How would you characterize the management style of your institution? Can it be described easily and consistently or does it tend toward inconsistency? Is it collaborative or is it combative? Is there a need for consensus or are decisions made and imposed? The way the management function of an institution works can provide a number of clues as to how you need to structure your enrollment management team. You can build your team quite differently depending on whether your institution's style is one of imposition from the top or whether you must be conscious of building campuswide consensus. The first will give you a great degree of latitude as to who and what you include but may not guarantee the levels of support you are seeking. The second will ensure a high degree of support but may make your team less coherent and focused than is desired. The management style of the institution will probably determine how you should approach building and structuring your team. However, it does not have to be the management style employed by the team. The management style you desire for the team should be seriously considered as you select the players.

Skills. Once an institution has set its strategy, established its shared values, made an assessment of the status and needs of its systems and procedures, and gained an understanding of the role its management style will play, it is in a position to outline the skills needed on its team to achieve the enrollment management objectives and evaluate the degree to which they are

currently available on the campus. Do you need skills in planning and evaluation, recruitment and retention, advising and placement? Although simply described and, presumably, readily understood, the determination and assessment of skills is not necessarily as easy as it may appear. Do you know what skills you really need? You may find that you will want to return to the question of needed skills at some point after you have basically structured your team and it has had an opportunity to consider the task before it. Your initial delineation of skills, however, is sufficient to lead you to the next team-building consideration.

Staff. Most of the skills deemed necessary to your enrollment management effort will be demonstrated through people. Note the use of the word *most.* The technology that affects our lives in geometrically progressive ways has already created machines that have some of the skills useful to enrollment management. The future undoubtedly holds many other surprises for us, but we cannot sit and wait. The challenge for the enrollment management team builder is to seek out people who possess the skills determined necessary. Are there people on your campus with the skills necessary to put together an institution-wide marketing plan? Are there people who have the knowledge and skills necessary to carry out the kind of research you will need? Do you have someone with a broad enough understanding of the elements you wish to include, as well as the management skills necessary, to lead your enrollment management operation? Our campuses have a great many talented and highly skilled people at work on them. The temptation, however, is to look at titles rather than abilities and, thus, often to overlook those with greater potential for contribution. Organizing for enrollment management is not something an institution undertakes casually and without expectation. The people who are selected to provide leadership as members of the enrollment management team must be the very best the institution can employ. There must be a concerted effort to avoid appointments that are simply used to reward or that satisfy a desire for reflected representation. Most importantly, the people selected must be ready to lead.

Structure. How an organization is structured may be the most important factor in its success. Structure alone, however, will not guarantee success. To create a structure without grounding it in a foundation might be analogous to building a pyramid that stands on its point. It can be done, but only a few are capable of engineering it! As recognized earlier, there is no one particular organizational structure for enrollment management that can be implanted on every campus. In fact, without a fairly detailed knowledge of the institution involved, it is even difficult to suggest an appropriate organizational model. You might find it useful to think of the organizational structure as dynamic rather than static and expect that it will evolve over time as the institution matures in its understanding and expectations of enrollment management. If you have thoroughly considered the previous *S*'s, the structure of your enrollment management team may be evident already.

Opportunity and Challenge

This chapter has not provided a prescription for how to organize your enrollment management team; that is something you and your institution need to consider. It has, however, outlined a variety of ideas that should lead you to some conclusions regarding how you might approach it. Enrollment management as it has been presented in this volume is much more than the latest administrative fashion; it is a theoretically grounded and integrated strategy for institutional vitality. If you are in the position of considering how to organize an enrollment management team, you have an opportunity to make a significant contribution to higher education. You are also facing a challenge that is not without risk. The way enrollment management is organized on your campus can and will affect the future of your institution and the students it exists to serve. I hope that when you have finished, you can relate to this comment attributed to a mythical college president (Trachtenberg, 1984, p. 12): "I have left no stone unturned and no heart unmoved in the struggle to see to it that our enrollments are managed at the very highest levels of competence . . . and that all of us at this school are enjoying the taste, sweeter than honeydew, of luscious, incomparable success."

References

Ambler, D. A. "The Administrative Role." In U. Delworth, G. R. Hanson, and Associates, *Student Services: A Handbook for the Profession.* San Francisco: Jossey-Bass, 1980.

Braxton, J. M. "Institutional Research: The Agenda." Paper presented at the Chicago Conference—Leadership for Enrollment Management, Chicago, July 1984.

Chatham, W. "Enrollment Management: A Community College Approach." Paper presented at the Second Chicago Conference—Leadership for Enrollment Management, Chicago, July 1985.

Cohen, M. D., and March, J. G. *Leadership and Ambiguity: The American College President.* New York: McGraw-Hill, 1974.

Davis-Van Atta, D. "Institutional Research: The Agenda." Paper presented at the Second Chicago Conference—Leadership for Enrollment Management, Chicago, July 1985.

Dutton, T. B., and Rickard, S. T. "Organizing Student Services." In U. Delworth, G. R. Hanson, and Associates, *Student Services: A Handbook for the Profession.* San Francisco: Jossey-Bass, 1980.

Graff, A. S. "Enrollment Management: Today and Tomorrow." Paper presented at the Second Chicago Conference—Leadership for Enrollment Management, Chicago, July 1985.

Hossler, D. R. *Enrollment Management: An Integrated Approach.* New York: The College Board, 1984.

Huddleston, T. "Effective Organizational Structure for Enrollment Management." Paper presented at the Chicago Conference—Leadership for Enrollment Management, Chicago, July 1984.

Johnstone, D. B., and Huff, R. P. "Relationship of Student Aid to Other College Programs and Services. " In R. H. Fenske, R. P. Hull, and Associates, *Handbook of Student Financial Aid: Programs, Procedures, and Policies.* San Francisco: Jossey-Bass, 1983.

Keller, G. "Enrollment Management: The Leadership Role." Paper presented at the Second Chicago Conference—Leadership for Enrollment Management, Chicago, July 1985.

Kemerer, F. R., Baldridge, J. V., and Green, K. C. *Strategies for Effective Enrollment Management.* Washington, D.C.: American Association of State Colleges and Universities, 1982.

Kennedy, A. M. "Developing an Effective Enrollment Management Approach for Small Colleges." Paper presented at the Chicago Conference—Leadership for Enrollment Management, Chicago, July 1984.

Kreutner, L., and Godfrey, E. S. "Enrollment Management: A New Vehicle for Institutional Renewal." *The College Board Review,* 1980-81, *118,* 6-9, 29.

Manski, C. F., and Wise, D. A. *College Choice in America.* Cambridge, Mass.: Harvard University Press, 1983.

Miller, T. K., and Prince, J. S. *The Future of Student Affairs: A Guide to Student Development for Tomorrow's Higher Education.* San Francisco: Jossey-Bass, 1976.

Novak, T., and Weiss, D. "What's All This Talk About Enrollment Management?" *The Admissions Strategist: Recruiting in the 1980s,* 1985, *4,* 1-5.

Peters, T. J., and Waterman, R. H., Jr. *In Search of Excellence: Lessons from America's Best-Run Companies.* New York: Harper & Row, 1982.

Rainsford, G. N. "Enrollment Management from a President's Perspective." *College and University,* 1985, *60* (4), 336-344.

Tierney, M. "Enrollment Planning and Management: New Challenges and New Opportunities." Paper presented at the Second Chicago Conference—Leadership for Enrollment Management, Chicago, July 1985.

Trachtenberg, S. J. "No Stone Unturned and No Heart Unmoved." Paper presented at the Chicago Conference—Leadership for Enrollment Management, Chicago, July 1984.

Zemsky, R., and Oedel, P. *The Structure of College Choice.* New York: College Entrance Examination Board, 1983.

A. Steven Graff is the director for admissions and guidance services in the Midwestern Regional Office of the College Board.

Enrollment management requires both broad perspectives and focus to be successful.

An Integrated Enrollment Management System

Marian Allen Claffey
Don Hossler

Institutional adaptation is almost a contradiction in terms, but that is what will be needed in the coming decade from institutions of higher education. As has been mentioned many times already, enrollment management offers higher education a significant opportunity to exert more control over an increasingly uncertain future. Key to the success of this attempt at adaptation will be the higher education administrator's *conceptual* understanding and acceptance of enrollment management, as well as the leadership implied in its implementation. Too often, the temptation is to trivialize the essence of enrollment management so that its utility is lost in the rush to implement new titles and new tactics. But if the opportunity is lost, it may never be realized or seized on again.

Thus, the purposes of this summary chapter are threefold: first, to provide two analogies for enrollment management so that the concept may be more easily shared with others; second, to describe the characteristics of the organizational climate that will be most effective in ensuring the success of an enrollment management strategy; and third, to discuss the integration of the system so that enrollments can be influenced.

D. Hossler (Ed.), *Managing College Enrollments*. New Directions for
Higher Education, no. 53. San Francisco: Jossey-Bass, March 1986.

The Enrollment Management Perspective

Like the lens of the eye or the lens of a camera, the enrollment manager's vision must adjust to the varying institutional images or situations presented. Some situations will require a broad, inclusive vision; others will require the ability to narrow the focus. Additionally, the enrollment manager must be able to turn the lens inward at the institution and look objectively—and critically—at the self-portrait that is captured. The true enrollment management system will be driven by the creativity and adaptability of this vision.

The Wide-Angle Lens. Higher education administrators are not usually in the habit of considering the "big picture" presented by their institutions while performing their jobs, neither are they always expected to do so. (The one exception might be during the preparation of budgets, when everyone is asked to "tighten the belt" for the benefit of the entire school.) Administrators in institutions of higher education (IHEs), typically having a particular division or function for which they are responsible, must routinely narrow their focus out of necessity rather than choice.

The president, more than anyone, ought to see the big picture. Too often, though, presidents must devote much of their attention to fiscal management, fund raising, and settling differences between competing constituencies within and outside of the institution. The enrollment manager or enrollment management team, however, deliberately and systematically looks at the IHE in its entirety; it looks at offices, services, and personnel that, although separate, fit naturally together. Thus, it looks for potential harmony from apparent cacophony. The enrollment manager, like an artist-photographer composing a shot that calls for a breadth of vision, looks at the institution through a wide-angle lens.

The Zoom Lens. An effective enrollment manager sees the big picture and can view the institution (and the external environment) through a wide-angle lens. He or she appreciates the seemingly disparate array of elements that converge on the student *prior* to enrollment. Conversely, the effective enrollment manager never loses sight of the divergent effects of matriculation and persistence of the student, and the student's impact on the institution.

It is as though the enrollment manager, while viewing the panorama of the student experience, periodically freezes the frame in order to change lenses and "zoom" in on the student. By focusing on the student at regular intervals, the enrollment manager is afforded the opportunity of checking the accuracy of his or her vision. The enrollment management perspective, though, requires the ability to revert back to the wide-angle lens in order to observe the variety of ways in which the student influences the institution.

Accommodating the Vision. The process of enrollment is cyclical in nature. In its most rudimentary form, it involves a cycle of the environment influencing the student and the student influencing the environment. The enrollment management perspective requires a continual widening and narrowing of the vision, the appropriateness of which is determined by the stage of the cycle being viewed.

Both the wide-angle and zoom lens analogies can be used, for example, to examine the impact of pricing and financial aid on enrollment. In the first stage, a variety of factors (wide-angle lens) impinge on the student's perceptions of a college and its affordability. If an IHE is to understand and influence the "student consumer," its perspective must be widened so as not to overlook and exclude these various factors.

During the second stage, this same student's persistence at a given school becomes a function of many factors, not the least of which may be financial. The enrollment manager must begin, however, to focus in on the determining factors (zoom lens) in order to establish the relative importance of financial considerations in the student's decision to persist.

In the third stage, the decision to persist has long-term effects for both the student and the institution. The range of effects, their implications, and their impact on students yet to come can best be understood by reverting back to a wide-angle lens. Enrollment management, then, involves a holistic view of the institution and the environment (wide-angle lens) and a focused view of the student (zoom lens).

Characteristics of the Organizational Climate

Much of the emphasis in this volume has been on functional definitions of enrollment management and specific activities that an IHE might employ in its implementation of an enrollment management plan. In Chapter Seven, on organizing for enrollment management, Graff makes reference to the dynamic characteristic of the components of an enrollment management system. It is to these dynamic characteristics that we now turn our attention.

The following are necessary conditions for effective enrollment management. Whether they are also sufficient depends on the individual institution.

- *The highest levels of administration are involved.* This is true in terms of both conceptual support and policy making. Strong leadership is always evident when enrollment management is working.
- *The vision is holistic.* As was mentioned in Chapter One, enrollment management is both a concept and a procedure; it demands a holistic vision of the institution and its mission, as well as a holistic view of students. It may very well mean seeing the various components of the IHE in completely new ways.
- *The stance is proactive.* Enrollment management is not merely an approach or a set of activities; it is a pervasive attitude that an institution has about itself and the way in which it intends to shape its future.
- *The decision making is informed.* The decision structures of a system may

be as idiosyncratic as the institution itself, as long as the decisions are informed. In addition, enrollment management does not shy away from making the "hard" decision, though it may involve ego, power, and turf—traditional forms of self-compensation in a social institution not known for its wealth.

- *The climate is flexible and tolerant.* Effective enrollment management allows for false starts, blind alleys, and experimentation. Mistakes are tolerated, but not more than once. It is understood that although there may be no one best model or ideal system, there may be synergistic effects from an individual model that are unique, unexpected, and rewarding.

Integrating the System

Attempting to synthesize the material in all of the preceding chapters may feel somewhat like experimenting with recombinant DNA: It is new, radical, risky, and possibly dramatic in its outcomes.

Davis-Van Atta and Carrier, in Chapter Six, describe enrollment management and institutional research as "an effective partnership." There are certainly other effective partnerships waiting to be forged in an experimental effort not unlike recombining DNA. Institutional research + retention, retention + outcomes, outcomes + marketing + recruitment, and so on are the most basic of formulas that will provide the foundation for an enrollment management system. The permutations that an IHE can conceive are limited only by the vision and imagination of that IHE.

Influencing Enrollments

Hossler (1984) has noted that collegiate enrollments may not actually be subject to management in the strictest sense and that *enrollment influencing* may be a more appropriate choice of terms. Planning and evaluation are at the heart of an enrollment management system, but the single most critical element in all of this effort is accurate, timely, usable information. Thus, our ability to influence our enrollments to any degree is a direct function of the information an IHE has available to itself. A colorful reflection on this notion can be found in Litten's chapter (Chapter Two) on pricing, as he notes: "Marketing without market research tends toward sorcery . . . market research without marketing is intellectual voyeurism."

"Information enables influence," according to Davis-Van Atta and Carrier. That is more than just an aphorism fit for a sampler; in higher education it is a truism for the 1980s and even through the end of the century, for the ability to influence enrollments may be the most that any institution can hope for.

Additional Topics Related to Enrollment Management

The topics related to enrollment management are too varied and extensive to provide a complete list of references in this sourcebook. The short list that follows represents some exemplary works in selected areas. For a more comprehensive reading list, consult the bibliographies of the following references:

Enrollment Management

Hossler, D. R. *Enrollment Management: An Integrated Approach.* New York: The College Board, 1984.
Kemerer, F. R., Baldridge, J. V., and Green, K. C. *Strategies for Effective Enrollment Management.* Washington, D.C.: American Association of State Colleges and Universities, 1982.

Pricing and Financial Aid

Kramer, M. (Ed.). *Meeting Student Aid Needs in a Period of Retrenchment.* New Directions for Higher Education, no. 40. San Francisco: Jossey-Bass, 1982.
Litten, L. H. (Ed.). *Issues in Pricing Undergraduate Education.* New Directions for Institutional Research, no. 42. San Francisco: Jossey-Bass, 1984.

Student Attrition

Pascarella, E. T. (Ed.). *Studying Student Attrition.* New Directions for Institutional Research, no. 36. San Francisco: Jossey-Bass, 1982.
Ramist, L. *College Student Attrition and Retention.* New York: College Entrance Examination Board, 1981.

Student College Choice

Litten, L. H., Sullivan, D., and Brodigan, D. L. *Applying Market Research in College Admissions.* New York: College Entrance Examination Board, 1983.
Zemsky, R., and Oedel, P. *The Structure of College Choice.* New York: College Entrance Examination Board, 1983.

Student-Institution Fit

Banning, J. H., and McKinley, D. L. "Conceptions of the Campus Environment." In W. H. Morrill, J. C. Hurst, and E. R. Oetting (Eds.), *Dimensions of Intervention for Student Development.* New York: Wiley, 1980.
Williams, T. E. "Recruiting Graduates: Understanding Student-Institution Fit." In D. R. Hossler (Ed.), *Enrollment Management: An Integrated Approach.* New York: The College Board, 1984.

Reference

Hossler, D. R. *Enrollment Management: An Integrated Approach.* New York: The College Board, 1984.

Marian Allen Claffey is assistant to the dean of the Graduate School, Loyola University of Chicago.

Don Hossler is assistant professor of higher education and student affairs at Indiana University, Bloomington.

Index